PSYCHOLOGY OF LEARNING AND DEVELOPMENT

DR. MUKTA GOYAL

Contents

Preface

The Master of Science in Learning and Development programme allows students to advance their knowledge and understanding of human development from infancy to adulthood while also gaining foundational knowledge in Educational Psychology.The psychology of learning is **a theoretical science that covers the various psychological theories that relate with learning**. Throughout history, there has been many various psychological learning theories. Some take on a more behaviorist approach which focuses on inputs and reinforcements.

The book containing the different viewpoints connecting with the brain science of learning and improvement of a youngster outfits legitimate comprehension to its perusers for aiding the developing kids in their thoroughgoing turn of events. The topic, capably isolated into many parts and coordinated in a rearranged and sensible way, first elucidates instructive brain science, improvement of the developing kids, cycle of learning, knowledge, fitness and demeanor, and afterward clarifies brain science of individual contrasts, learning styles, learning handicaps, imagination, character, emotional wellness, change, direction and guiding, and at last, gatherings and collective vibes.

The book is essentially intended for the post-graduate students of Education . The goal of this book is to provide current information and meet the urgent needs of students pursuing B.Ed, M.Ed, and B.A (Education) degrees and preparing for NET-JRF, SET, SLET, and other competitive exams.

After Reading this book, the student will be able to:

· acquaint the learner with the process of development and assessment and its implication in teaching learning process · develop an understanding of different stages of growth and development · explain the Piaget's concept of cognitive development · differentiate between Kohlberg's theory of moral development and Erikson theory of psycho-social development · gaining deep insight in to the theoretical Frameworks (psychological theories for education)of Learning, its management and their implication to better understand and bringing desirable modification in learner's behaviour · Differentiate between creativity and intelligence, their assessment and educational importance · Indentifying the ways of motivating the learner in classroom setting · Assess different types of techniques of personality and their teaching strategy according to needs of students. · analyze the importance of adjustment and its strategies in their day to day life.

We are hoping that this book meets all essential requirements, and that its widespread distribution will have a significant impact on educational theory.

Dr.Mukta Goyal

CHAPTER ONE

Education And Psychology

Introduction

Child Development

The early years of a child's life are very important for his or her health and development. Healthy development means that children of all abilities, including those with special health care needs, are able to grow up where their social, emotional, and educational needs are met. Having a safe and loving home and spending time with family—playing, singing, reading, and talking—are very important. Proper nutrition, exercise, and sleep also can make a big difference. Building on a well-established knowledge base more than half a century in the making, recent advances in the science of early childhood development and its underlying biology provide a deeper understanding that can inform and improve existing policy and practice, as well as help generate new ways of thinking about solutions

What is childhood?

To comprehend the concept of child growth, one must first comprehend the concepts of kid, childhood, and childlikeness. A child is a biological construct associated with the age range of 0 to 18. This age is also vulnerable to change based on a variety of social factors.

Childhood is a collection of activities that a child engages in from infancy to puberty. Childhood is a fluid concept with no universal meaning. Depending on social reality and developments that have occurred over time. Childhood is a social and cultural construct built around the child's activities.

Importance of childhood

Early childhood is said to play a role in a person's life achievement, research, and emotional well-being. We know that if we do it right and proper in the early years, children will thrive throughout their school years and adult lives.

Childhood is influenced by both nature and nurture (genes and environment). The quality of a child's early settings, as well as the availability of relevant experiences at the appropriate developmental time, are important factors in how each child's brain architecture develops.

The emotional, social, and physical development of children has a direct impact on their total development and on who they will become as adults. It is critical to recognize the importance of investing in children (beginning at a young age) in order to enhance their future well-being.

Meaning of Child Development

Child development is a specialized area of study which concerns itself the growth and development of a child right from the moment of conception to adolescence.

The term development means a progressive series of changes that occurs as a result of maturation and learning development implies qualitative changes. This means that development does not consist of adding inches to one's height or increasing kg in weight. These include changes in abilities like learning to speak, changes in behavior, interests, comprehension, etc.

According to Laura Berk, Child development is a field of study devoted to understanding human constancy and change from conception through adolescence.

Scope of Child Development

In your child's growth, especially in the early years, a well-balanced concentration on learning is critical. Child ventures‘ curriculum is made up of aspects from three different educational methods: Montessori, High Scope, and Core Knowledge. Each teaching style benefits your child's learning in a different way.

High Scope is a hands-on method that fosters active learning beginning in infancy and going throughout toddlerhood.

Here are eight ways the High Scope learning technique fosters child development for your little one, including abilities such as music, movement, numbers, and time:

Emphasizes Problem Solving skills: The High Scope technique emphasizes social and emotional development, which are important life skills for your child. Teachers encourage youngsters to carry out conflict resolution processes independently by addressing issues through a sequence of steps.

Encouraged Use of All Senses: High Scope activities differ depending on the group, age level, and school setting. Most activities include engaging several senses at once, with active, hands-on learning being the main proponent of High Scope activities.

Education Through Movement: Children have a natural need to move, sing, and play throughout their early years. This fact is used by High Scope to incorporate developmentally appropriate activities into its teaching methods.

Fosters Decision-Making Skills: Children in the High Scope programmed to have the freedom to pick what they want to do and how they want to learn on a daily basis.

Promotes Independence: Children's independence grows as they have the opportunity to strengthen decision-making abilities by selecting their own activities. They become less reliant on teachers to educate them during the day and instead search for answers.

Cultivates Curiosity: Children are encouraged to further investigate what hobbies interest them, similar to developing independence, with the guidance of their teachers. For example, if a child expresses an interest in mixing paint colors to produce new shades, the instructor will assist this activity by gathering resources.

Increases Confidence: The High Scope technique is designed to work for all pupils, regardless of their background or aptitude. Children build on their own abilities to design a learning path that suits and supports their particular learning interests.

Creates Social Relations: Interactions in a group setting, including small and big group experiences and activities, create crucial communication and social skills.

The High Scope technique has been integrated into the curriculum for the Infant and Toddler programmed at Child ventures. To learn more about the curriculum, please contact us.

Difference between Growth and Development

What is Growth? An increase in the size of an object or a live creature is referred to as growth. It's been used in phrases like "the lump has expanded in size." The term "growth" refers to the act of growing. As an example, 'the country's economy grew rapidly.' It denotes a rise in the worth of something. 'The number of hospitals in the city has increased.' Growth can refer to a rise in the size of a crop or the production of a particular fruit. 'The farmer was astounded by the incredible grape growth.'

The term "full growth" is used to describe a mature state. 'The investment has reached its full potential.' Any industry that is rapidly developing can be labeled as a "growth industry." The phrase 'steel industry is currently the growth industry' is an example of its application. A 'growth stock,' on the other hand, is one that tends to increase in capital value. This particular application is common in the stock market.

What is development? The term "development" refers to a rise in one's degree of functioning. It's been used in phrases like "he evolved into a nice cop." The term "development" can refer to an improvement in one's health. As an example, 'he now has a better pulse rate.'

The term "development" is used to describe the process of being developed or the act of developing. In fact, it is employed to communicate the concept of a "development stage." In a nutshell, the term "growth" can be considered a subset of the term "development." One of the clearest examples of its application is the phrase "the lump grew into a tumor due to an increase in its growth." The phrase "an increase in its growth" in this case denoted an increase in the lump's size. As a result, the term "growth" might be considered a subset of "development."

The term "development" can refer to a steady shift. The word "development" can be used to describe a development process. You may use something like, "the process of developing an image." A fully developed state or piece of land is an example of development. 'A developed portion of agricultural land,' 'a developed region of land,' and similar expressions are instances of this type of usage. The former word refers to fertility, but the latter phrase refers to an improvement in living conditions.

A 'development area' is an area where new industries are fostered in order to create jobs and stimulate the economy. The related use is: 'This country abounds in numerous development areas.' Take note of the phrase "the boy has matured into a lovely youth." This sentence alludes to the growth of his body's features. As a result, the meanings of the two words 'growth' and 'development' are vastly different.

Difference between Growth and Development

Growth is the process of something growing larger, longer, more numerous, or more important, which is usually a physical change; development is the process of something changing (usually for the better) into a new stage or improving, which can be physical, social, or psychological.

An increase in the size of an object or a live creature is referred to as growth. The term "development" refers to a rise in one's degree of functioning.

The term "growth" refers to the act of growing. It denotes a rise in the worth of something. Growth can refer to a rise in the size of a crop or the production of a particular fruit.

The term "development" can refer to an improvement in one's health. The term "development" can refer to a steady shift.

Interdisciplinary Basis of child development

Typically demanding a spark of creativity coupled with experimentation,

Interdisciplinary teaching can be an ambitious approach to use in your classroom.

Fortunately, there are activities you can implement relatively easily that deliver research-backed benefits. These include:

• Improved Critical Thinking — Students should improve their analysis abilities by using approaches from different disciplines.

• Better Bias Recognition — To solve a problem that demands an interdisciplinary approach, students must typically use information rooted in a range of perspectives. This can often challenge their pre-existing ideas to help them identify bias in themselves in others.

• Preparation for Future Problems — Using skills and knowledge from different disciplines is practice for solving problems outside school walls.

Framed by a definition and supplemented with unit design steps, below are 10 interdisciplinary teaching activities and examples. To choose ones that suit your schedule, they're categorized by length.

A Multidisciplinary Approach to Early Childhood Education and Care examines early childhood education and care in Australia from a variety of angles, emphasizing the field's complexity and the necessity for a truly interdisciplinary approach. It claims that only a comprehensive understanding of each viewpoint would allow for a clear future for early childhood education in Australia, and that all political parties should work together to improve policy and provision to assure the sector's support and development.

By exploring current government policies, as well as individual and communal initiatives, the chapters provide insights into how children and families are positioned in educational change. Positive, behavioral, developmental, economic, sociocultural, and postmodern models are among the paradigms studied. Garvis and Manning identify field issues and suggest modifications to assist establish an interdisciplinary approach to help decrease the educational outcomes disadvantage gap.

This book is supposed to stimulate considerable advances in early childhood education and care in Australia, with recommendations addressed at stakeholders from several disciplines. This book will stimulate new ways of thinking about policy and provision development for the future by providing crucial insights into the landscape of early childhood education and care.

From birth until age five, there are many opportunities and risks for healthy physical, emotional, social, and cognitive development

Human development is the consequence of a complicated interaction between genetic predispositions and environmental factors. Nature and nurture, both separately and in combination, play important roles throughout a person's existence. In particular, the first few years of life are a critical time throughout the development process, setting the groundwork for cognitive functioning, behavioral, social, and self-regulatory capacities, and physical health in childhood and beyond.

A lot of elements are important for optimal growth throughout these early years. They include the nature of early caregiver connections, the level of cognitive stimulation provided, and availability to proper nourishment and health care. Some children will be robust in the face of early childhood stressors, while others' healthy development will be jeopardized, with temporary or long-term consequences.

In the years leading up to school admission, a significant number of youngsters are exposed to dangers that may restrict their development

Living in poverty, being a single parent, and having a woman with less than a high school degree, among other factors, all increase the risk of developmental delay. Nearly half of a recent cohort of kindergarten students in the United States studied as part of the US Department of Education's Early Childhood Longitudinal Study of the Kindergarten Class of 1998–1999 (ECLS-K) experienced one or more of our risk factors. Nearly one in every six people was subjected to more than one type of abuse. Exposure to such dangers does not always result in developmental issues. Some youngsters are resilient, but the consequences for others can be severe.

Disparities in school preparedness result from differences in early childhood experiences, and these inequalities frequently endure

Early childhood disadvantages have ramifications for how prepared children are when they start school. School preparation includes not only cognitive abilities, but also those related to socializing, self-control, and learning styles.

While these readiness indicators suggest that children who grow up in more enriched surroundings are better prepared for school, longitudinal data show that these early gaps continue and even enlarge as children advance through school. As a result, achievement inequalities tend to increase over time as disadvantaged students do not progress at the same rate as their more advantaged peers.

Children from disadvantaged homes are also more likely to get special education, repeat grades, and drop out of high school. Lower levels of school achievement are linked to adverse life outcomes in later years. Low employment rates, welfare dependency, and delinquency and crime are examples of the latter. Even if only a part of these negative childhood and adult outcomes can be avoided, the advantages could be significant.

Early childhood interventions are intended to help children cope with a variety of stressors while also promoting healthy growth

Early childhood interventions are intended to act as a buffer against the many risk factors that may jeopardize a child's healthy development in the years leading up to school enrollment. While they all have the same goal, early childhood interventions use a wide range of approaches; there is no one-size-fits-all approach. Programs differ in terms of the results they seek to achieve and the risk factors they examine when determining eligibility, such as poor socioeconomic position and single parenthood.

They differ in terms of whether they are directed at the child, the parent, or both, as well as the level of personalized attention they provide. Different programmers cater to children of all ages and differ in terms of the services they provide, where they are provided, and how many hours per week they are provided.

Early childhood therapies that are rigorously evaluated can help us understand what outcomes they may enhance

Although we may anticipate positive outcomes from early childhood programmers, a scientifically solid review is essential to determine whether they deliver on their promise. Because of the wide range of early childhood intervention approaches, such evaluations are required across the entire spectrum of program models, ideally with the ability to determine the effects of changing key program characteristics.

While numerous early childhood interventions have been adopted and some have been evaluated in some way, only a small percentage have been evaluated using scientifically sound methodologies. We found published evaluations for 20 early childhood programs with well-implemented experimental designs or strong quasi-experimental designs after researching the literature on studies of early childhood interventions that matched our criteria for rigorous assessment.

Some initiatives were omitted from the list because their evaluations did not fulfil minimal scientific rigor standards (e.g., a large enough sample size). Sixteen programs had the most evidence since they tracked results from kindergarten admission to graduation.

Stages of Development

Prenatal Development

How did you become the person you are today? Your prenatal development took place in an ordered and delicate sequence, beginning as a single cell structure and ending with your birth.

Prenatal development is divided into three stages: germinal, embryonic, and fetal. Let's take a look at what the developing infant goes through at each of these stages.

Germinal Stage (Weeks 1- 2)

You learned about genetics and DNA during the earlier topic of biopsychology in the book. At the moment of conception, the DNA of the mother and father is passed on to the kid. When sperm fertilizes an egg and generates a zygote, it is called conception. When sperm and egg combine, a zygote is formed as a one-cell structure. At this phase, the baby's genetic makeup and sex are determined. The zygote divides and multiplies during the first week following conception, going from a one-cell structure to two cells, four cells, eight cells, and so on. Mitosis is the name given to the process of cell division.

Mitosis is a delicate process, with only about half of all zygotes surviving past the first two weeks (Hall, 2004). There are 100 cells after 5 days of mitosis, and billions of cells after 9 months. As cells divide, they become more specialized, resulting in the formation of various organs and body components. The mass of cells has not yet attached themselves to the lining of the mother's uterus in the germinal stage. The following stage begins after that.

Embryonic Stage (Weeks 3- 8)

The zygote goes down the fallopian tubes and inserts itself in the uterine lining after dividing for 7–10 days and having 150 cells. This multicellular organism is referred to as an embryo once it has been implanted. The placenta is now formed by the growth of blood vessels. The placenta is a uterine structure that transports nutrients and oxygen from the mother to the developing embryo via the umbilical cord.

The embryo's basic structures begin to form the sections that will become the head, chest, and abdomen. The heart begins to beat and organs build and function during the embryonic stage. The neural tube develops into the spinal cord and brain along the back of the embryo.

Fetal Stage (Weeks 9- 40)

The embryo is known as a fetus when it is about nine weeks old. The fetus is approximately the size of a kidney bean at this point, and it's starting to take on the shape of a human being when the "tail" fades away.

The sex organs begin to distinguish between 9 and 12 weeks. The fetus is around 4.5 inches long at 16 weeks. Fingers and toes are fully formed, with visible fingerprints. The fetus can weigh up to 1.4 pounds by the time it reaches the sixth month of development (24 weeks). The fetus' hearing has matured to the point that it can respond to sounds. Internal organs such as the lungs, heart, stomach, and intestines have matured to the degree where a prematurely born fetus can survive outside the mother's womb.

The brain continues to grow and develop throughout the prenatal stage, approximately doubling in size from weeks 16 to 28. The fetus is almost ready to be born at 36 weeks. By week 37, all of the fetus' organ systems have developed to the point where it may survive outside the mother's uterus without many of the hazards associated with preterm birth. Until the fetus reaches 40 weeks, it continues to acquire weight and length. The fetus has very little room to move around by this time, and birth is imminent.

Influences During Pregnancy

Genetic and environmental factors can influence development at each prenatal stage. The developing fetus is totally reliant on the mother for survival. It is critical that the mother takes care of herself and receives prenatal care, which is medical care provided during pregnancy that monitors both the mother and the fetus's health.

From Infancy to Childhood

A newborn weighs about 7.5 pounds on average. A newborn, despite his small size, is not completely helpless because his reflexes and sensory abilities enable him to interact with his surroundings from birth. Every healthy baby is born with newborn reflexes, which are inborn automatic responses to specific types of stimulation. Reflexes help the newborn survive until it is able to perform more complex behaviors—these reflexes are critical for survival. They appear in babies whose brains are developing normally and usually disappear around the age of 4–5 months. Let's look at a few of these newborn reflexes. The rooting reflex is the newborn's reaction to anything that moves. When you stroke a baby's cheek, she naturally turns her head in that direction and starts sucking. The sucking reflex refers to the automatic, unlearned sucking motions performed by infants with their mouths. Several other fascinating newborn reflexes can be seen. For example, if you insert your finger into a newborn's hand, you will observe the grasping reflex, in which a baby automatically grasps anything that comes into contact with his palms. The Moro reflex is the newborn's reaction when she feels she is about to fall. The baby spreads her arms, then pulls them in, and (usually) cries. How do you believe these reflexes aid in survival during the first few months of life?

Physical Growth and Development

The physical development of the body is rapid during infancy, toddlerhood, and early childhood ([link]). Newborns weigh between 5 and 10 pounds on average, and their weight doubles in six months and triples in a year. Weight will have quadrupled by the age of two, so a two-year-old should weigh between 20 and 40 pounds. A newborn's average length is 19.5 inches, increasing to 29.5 inches at 12 months and 34.4 inches at 2 years old (WHO Multicentre Growth Reference Study Group, 2006).

Motor development occurs in an orderly sequence as infants move from reflexive reactions (e.g., sucking and rooting) to more advanced motor functioning. For instance, babies first learn to hold their heads up, then to sit with assistance, and then to sit unassisted, followed later by crawling and then walking.

Our ability to move our bodies and manipulate objects is referred to as Motor Skills. Fine motor skills are the muscles in our fingers, toes, and eyes that allow us to coordinate small actions (e.g., grasping a toy, writing with a pencil, and using a spoon). Gross motor skills are concerned with large muscle groups that control our arms and legs, as well as larger movements (e.g., balancing, running, and jumping).

Development of the Mind(Cognitive Development)

Young children exhibit significant development of their cognitive abilities in addition to rapid physical growth. Piaget believed that children's ability to understand objects, such as learning that a rattle makes a noise when shaken, is a cognitive skill that develops gradually as a child grows and interacts with his or her environment. Today, developmental psychologists believe Piaget was mistaken. Researchers discovered that even very young children understand objects and how they work long before they have any experience with them (Baillargeon, 1987; Baillargeon, Li, Gertner, & Wu, 2011).

There are cognitive milestones that we expect children to reach, just as there are physical milestones. It is beneficial to be aware of these developmental milestones as children develop new abilities to think, problem-solve, and communicate. For example, around 6–9 months, infants shake their heads "no," and around 9–12 months, they respond to verbal requests to do things like "wave bye-bye" or "blow a kiss." Remember Piaget's theories on object permanence? We can expect children to understand that objects continue to exist even when they are not visible by the age of 8 months. Toddlers (those aged 12–24 months) enjoy games like hiding and seek because they have mastered object permanence which recognizes that when someone leaves the room, they will return (Loop, 2013). When asked to find objects, toddlers will point to pictures in books and look at inappropriate places.

At this age, children undergo a significant cognitive change. Remember that Piaget labeled 2–3-year-olds as egocentric, which means they are unaware of the perspectives of others. Children between the ages of 3 and 5 begin to understand that other people have thoughts, feelings, and beliefs that differ from their own. This is referred to as theory-of-mind (TOM).

Attachment

Children's psychosocial development occurs as they form relationships, interact with others, and learn to understand and manage their emotions. Forming healthy attachments is a major social milestone of infancy in terms of social and emotional development. Attachment is a long-term connection or bond with another person. Developmental psychologists are curious about how infants achieve this milestone. They inquire, for example, "How do parent-infant attachment bonds form?" What effect does neglect have on these bonds? What factors contribute to children's attachment differences?

Self-Concept

The development of a positive sense of self is the primary psychosocial milestone of childhood, just as attachment is the primary psychosocial milestone of infancy. What factors influence the development of self-awareness? Infants lack a self-concept, or understanding of who they are. If you put a baby in front of a mirror, she will reach out to touch her reflection, believing it is another baby. A toddler, on the other hand, will recognize herself in the mirror by the age of 18 months. What evidence do we have?

In a well-known experiment, a researcher painted a red dot on the noses of children before placing them in front of a mirror (Amsterdam, 1972).

The formation of a positive self-concept is essential for healthy development. Children who have a positive self-concept are more confident, perform better in school, act independently, and are more willing to try new things (Maccoby, 1980; Ferrer & Fugate, 2003). The development of a positive self-concept begins in Erikson's toddlerhood stage when children gain autonomy and confidence in their abilities. When children compare themselves to others in elementary school, they continue to develop their self-concept.

Stages of Adolescence

Adolescence is the time when a person transitions from childhood to adulthood. It involves significant physical and psychological changes in a young person's life. Both children and their families may experience excitement and worry as a result of the numerous physical, sexual, cognitive, social, and emotional changes that occur during this period. Understanding what to expect at different stages of adolescence and early adulthood might help to encourage healthy development.

Early adolescence (Ages 10 to 13)

Children often begin to grow faster at this age. They also start to notice other physical changes, such as hair growth under the arms and near the genitals, female breast development, and male testicular enlargement. They typically begin a year or two earlier in girls than in boys, and some changes can occur as early as age 8 in females and age 9 in males. Many girls begin their periods at the age of twelve, about two to three years after the onset of breast growth.

Some people may be both curious and anxious about these changes in their bodies, especially if they are unsure of what to anticipate or what is normal. At this age, some children may begin to question their gender identity, and puberty can be a challenging time for transgender youngsters.

Early teenage thought is definite and black-and-white. Without many areas in between, things are either right or bad, amazing or dreadful. It's natural for young people to focus their thoughts on themselves at this age (called "egocentrism"). As a result, preteens and early adolescent girls and boys are frequently self-conscious about their appearance and believe that they are constantly being scrutinized by their classmates.

Pre-teens have a stronger desire for seclusion. They may begin to look for ways to be self-sufficient from their family. They may push boundaries during this process, and if parents or guardians reinforce restrictions, they may react violently.

Middle Adolescence (Ages 14 to 17)

During middle adolescence, physical changes from puberty continue. The majority of males will have begun their growth spurt, and puberty-related changes will be ongoing. As their voices fall, they may experience some vocal cracking. Acne affects some people. Females' physical transformations may be practically complete, and most girls now have regular periods.

Many teenagers grow interested in romantic and sexual relationships at this age. They may doubt and explore their sexual identity, which can be difficult if they do not have peer, family, or community support. Self-stimulation, often known as masturbation, is another common approach for the youth of all genders to explore sex and sexuality.

As they strive for more independence, many middle teens have more disagreements with their parents. They may spend more time with friends and less time with relatives. They are particularly conscious of their appearance, and peer pressure is likely to be at its greatest at this age.

In this period, the brain continues to evolve and mature, but there are still numerous distinctions between how a normal middle adolescent thinks and how an adult thinks. Much of this is due to the fact that the frontal lobes are the last portions of the brain to mature, and development does not end until well into one's twenties! The frontal lobes are important for complicated decision-making, impulse control, and the ability to weigh various options and consequences. Middle teenagers are better at thinking abstractly and considering "the big picture," but they may still be unable to apply it in the present.

Late Adolescence (Age 18- 21 and beyond):

Late teenagers have reached the full adult height and have completed their physical development. By this time, they should have more impulse control and be able to accurately assess risks and rewards. Teenagers approaching early adulthood have a deeper sense of self-identity and are able to identify their own ideals. They may become more future-oriented, making judgments based on their ambitions and beliefs. Friendships and romantic relationships become more stable as a result of these changes.

They grow emotionally and physically estranged from their loved ones. Many people, on the other hand, re-establish an "adult" relationship with their parents, seeing them as more of a peer with whom to seek advice and discuss mature issues rather than an authority figure.

Domains of Development

Living and learning go hand in hand from birth to death. Nothing, however, compares to our first few years of life, when we learn to walk, talk, and interact with other people and our surroundings, as well as process how these activities make us feel. Although children develop at varying speeds, there are a number of crucial developmental milestones that each individual should achieve.

Early intervention treatments can be used to try to minimize or limit the impact of a suspected intellectual or developmental handicap once a defect has been identified.

A child must either obtain a qualifying diagnosis (such as autism) or show a 25% or greater delay in one or more of the five categories of development to be eligible for early intervention. Physical, cognitive, linguistic, socio-emotional, and adaptive abilities are among them. Let's look at each of these areas to see what they entail and what to look for.

Physical: A child must either obtain a qualifying diagnosis (such as autism) or show a 25% or greater delay in one or more of the five categories of development to be eligible for early intervention. Physical, cognitive, linguistic, socio-emotional, and adaptive abilities are among them. Let's look at each of these areas to see what they entail and what to look for.

Humans acquire physical ability in three directions: top to bottom, center to the periphery, and center to the periphery. As a baby grows older, he or she will be able to swivel their head and sit upright, before reaching, grabbing, and finally walking and running (2-3 years). During this time, the infant should be able to respond and react spontaneously to stimuli in his or her physical environment.

Cognitive: The ability to mentally digest information - to think, reason, and understand what's going on around you — falls under the cognitive domain of development. Jean Piaget, a developmental psychologist, separated cognitive development into four stages.

Humans are primarily limited to seeing the world on a sensory level throughout the sensorimotor stage of cognitive development (0-2 years). And the grownup makes a wry expression at you? Make a fool of yourself by laughing at what you see. Is there a toy dangling in front of you? Make a grab for it.

When a child reaches the preoperational stage (2-6 years), he or she begins to employ language in their study of people and their surroundings.

In most situations, though, logical functioning isn't quite there yet, and the youngster may struggle to "put it all together."

Prior to puberty, a kid should have reached the concrete operational stage (7-11 years), at which point he or she can comprehend events and information at face value but cannot handle abstracts or hypotheticals.

People aged 12 and up are said to be in the formal operational stage, capable of performing the complex mental gymnastics that distinguish humans. Abstract thinking, such as imagining hypothetical scenarios, formulating plans, and sorting through various points of view, becomes a regular aspect of dealing with reality.

Communicative: Understanding, utilizing, and manipulating language may be the single most powerful skill a person can acquire. Phonology (the formation of a language's constituent sounds into words), syntax (the fitting of those words together into sentences according to a language's rules and conventions), semantics (meaning and shades of meaning), and pragmatics (the use of language) are the four aspects of language development (how the language is applied in practical and interpersonal communication). Individuals' verbal communication skills vary greatly, but by the age of two, many toddlers are capable of at least telegraphic speech, which consists of brief words that communicate the core of a wish or need.

Socioemotional: To truly thrive, we must learn to interact with others and exist happily inside ourselves. As a child matures in the socioemotional realm, he or she learns to successfully manage his or her own internal emotional state as well as interpret others' social signs. Strong emotions can be properly controlled or communicated; confrontations may be handled without resorting to violence, and we can learn to empathize with others.

A baby should be reacting to facial expressions and reciprocating by the age of six months.

By a year, obvious preferences in terms of likes and dislikes, as well as recognition of the familiar vs the unknown, should have emerged.

A kid should be participating in parallel play with his or her peers by the age of two. Even though each child is engaged in a different activity, they are interested in and comfortable in each other's company.

By three years, self-awareness and the ability to communicate sentiments should have developed.

The child should be able to work cooperatively with others, follow simple rules, and manage emotions without tantrums or aggressiveness by the age of four.

Adaptive: Adaptive development refers to the aspect of growing up that involves self-care, such as eating, drinking, toileting, bathing, and dressing oneself. It also requires being aware of one's surroundings and any potential threats, as well as keeping oneself safe and secure. Before his or her fourth birthday, a kid should have made significant growth in these areas.

Role of Heredity, Environment, Maturation, and Learning in Children's Development

Role of Heredity and Development:

Meaning of Heredity:

Each person has a unique set of actions and personality traits. The influence of heredity and environment is visible in this disparity. Indeed, heredity and environment play a significant effect in the development of a person's personality and other characteristics.

Without heredity, no one can be born, and genes cannot grow properly without the right environment. From the moment of conception, an individual's heredity is there, and some external conditions begin to influence him at this period as well.

An individual's heredity is determined by his parents' genes, which means that whatever one contributes to his children is passed down through the genes. The mechanism of heredity is detailed in the following section:

Mechanism of Heredity:

Mating: The first step in reproduction is mating. The zygote is the outcome of the combination of male sperm and female ovum.

Growth: The fertilized cell or zygote is divided several times.

chromosomes: Every woman and male inherit 23 chromosomes from each parent, for a total of 46 chromosomes.

Genes: Each chromosome is made up of microscopic particles called genes that range in size from 40 to 100.

Chance Factor: Both the ovum and the sperm have 23 pairs of chromosomes before fertilization. The genes in the sperm's chromosomes pair with the genes in the ovum during conception, determining the offspring's potential characteristics and qualities.

Meaning of Environment

The term "environment" refers to the whole of a person's surroundings in which he or she must live. An individual's environment is psychologically linked to all of the stimuli he encounters from conception to death. Natural and social environments are the two main types of environments. All of the things and forces on and around the earth that influence a person are referred to as the natural environment.

We mean the environment that a person perceives around him when he first becomes aware of society, such as language, religion, custom, tradition, means of communication, means of luxury, family, school, social groups, and so on.

Educational Implications of Heredity and Environment

Human development is greatly influenced by knowledge of heredity and the environment. Human growth is influenced by both genes and the surrounding environment. Children's growth patterns are influenced by both inheritance and environment.

The educational pattern, methods, and learning environment should be created by the instructor in the teaching-learning scenario based on the developmental pattern of the children. As a result, understanding heredity and environment benefit the teacher in a variety of ways, which are addressed further below.

Knowledge of genetics and the environment aids the teacher in understanding the children's various needs and talents.

It assists him in providing suitable educational, vocational, and personal direction to his children.

It aids the teacher in classifying children as talented, average, or slow learners and assigning them to different types of schooling.

It aids the teacher in creating a more conducive learning atmosphere in the classroom.

It aids the instructor in understanding the idea of individual variations and arranging the educational experience appropriately.

Role of Maturation and Learning in Children's Life

By their very nature, all living things or organisms go through a maturing process. Humans are special in that while they age, they also go through the process of learning through cognition, making maturation and learning intertwined. So, what exactly is maturation? What exactly is learning? What function does maturation play in learning if they are intertwined?

A newborn baby is the world's most helpless creature. His head is far too big for his body. His legs and feet are too small for him. He is unable to stand or even hold his head up. His hands are unsuitable for any skill. He doesn't have any teeth. His voice is audible, but it is monotonous for human speech. He has eyes and ears, but he never uses them. He sleeps the majority of the time. Despite his large head, his brain appears to be inactive.

The baby, on the other hand, is capable of development. He possesses the ability to grow. His legs and hands grow to the length of a human being. His muscles develop to the size and strength required for standing, walking, and running. His teeth were already present in rudimentary form.

At the appropriate ages, his form will grow, harden, and breakthrough his gums. His mouth and larynx develop into adaptable speech organs. His brain will not only grow in size but also in the fineness of its microscopic structure, allowing it to participate in a variety of human activities. The transition of an organism from an immature to a mature state is referred to as maturation.

If it were possible to accelerate a child's development and have it completed in a single week, would that week-old grown-up be a true adult, a competent adult? It would be impossible for him to learn much about the world in a week, let alone master the language and the thousands of skilful acts that adults are expected to perform. For this, we must add to the power of growth another important capacity which may be called the power of learning.

Learning: Learning, according to William Huitt, is the generally permanent change in an individual's conduct or potential behavior as a result of practice experience. Learning, according to Schunk, is a long-term change in behavior or the capacity to behave in a certain way that occurs as a result of practice or other forms of experience. We can draw from these definitions that three factors are present in learning: change, persistence, and the result of experience or practice.

These are the three events that makeup learning. Change, Endurance across time, and Consequence of Experience is, in fact, Schunk's three core requirements for what constitutes learning. Learning, in my opinion, is a process that begins with the learner acquiring stimuli from his or her environment, whether through experience or instruction, and culminates in a lasting change in the learner's behavior, abilities, or wisdom through cognition or mental processes. This adjustment must be long-lasting; else, there will be no learning.

Maturation: Unlike maturity, which is the outcome of biological growth and development, learning (Huitt) is a psychological process. Maturation is a natural process that occurs without human involvement. Learning occurs when a person's intellect interacts with his physical and social environment. Maturation and learning, on the other hand, are linked. As a person ages, so does his or her knowledge, talents, and attitude. A youngster learns only the most fundamental things, but as he grows older, his knowledge expands, allowing him to learn more complex things. It is critical that teachers keep this link in mind.

Teachers must understand the learner's maturity and psychological capability in order to establish learning strategies and materials that are appropriate for the learner's maturity level. The students in the classroom have varying levels of maturity and ability. If the lessons given are beyond a child's age range, he or she will be disappointed. On the other hand, if insufficient is provided, the opportunity to develop a child's potential is squandered. The attention span of children is one example. Children have a limited attention span, and if this isn't factored into the teacher's teaching technique, a lot of the teachings will be wasted.

Thus, we can say that Learning is critical for acquiring new knowledge, skills, and attitudes required for a successful life. Growing and learning are equally important. According to Woodworth and Marquis, "while many animals reach maturity in a few weeks or months after birth, the human being takes about 18 years, and during all of these years he is learning." What he is as an adult is determined by how well he has matured and what he has learned."

Maturation and learning go hand in hand in the process of human development; the growth of the structures of the body allows for the performance of various activities, and these activities allow for the performance of learning. The majority of the abilities of the adult are, "therefore, dependent on both maturation and learning. There are some abilities that do not depend on learning.

Suggested Readings:

Brookshaw, S. (2009). The material culture of children and childhood: Understanding childhood objects in the museum context. Journal of Material Culture, 14(3), 365-383.

Ginsburg, I. (1982). Jean Piaget and Rudolf Steiner: Stages of child development and implications for pedagogy. Teachers College Record, 84(2), 327-337.

Bijou, S. W. (1976). Child development: The basic stage of early childhood.

Pem, D. (2015). Factors affecting early childhood growth and development: Golden 1000 days. Adv Practice Nurs, 1(101), 2573-0347.

CHAPTER TWO

Growth and Development

Introduction

Child Development

The early years of a child's life are very important for his or her health and development. Healthy development means that children of all abilities, including those with special health care needs, are able to grow up where their social, emotional, and educational needs are met. Having a safe and loving home and spending time with family—playing, singing, reading, and talking—are very important. Proper nutrition, exercise, and sleep also can make a big difference. Building on a well-established knowledge base more than half a century in the making, recent advances in the science of early childhood development and its underlying biology provide a deeper understanding that can inform and improve existing policy and practice, as well as help generate new ways of thinking about solutions

What is childhood?

To comprehend the concept of child growth, one must first comprehend the concepts of kid, childhood, and childlikeness. A child is a biological construct associated with the age range of 0 to 18. This age is also vulnerable to change based on a variety of social factors.

Childhood is a collection of activities that a child engages in from infancy to puberty. Childhood is a fluid concept with no universal meaning. Depending on social reality and developments that have occurred over time. Childhood is a social and cultural construct built around the child's activities.

Importance of childhood

Early childhood is said to play a role in a person's life achievement, research, and emotional well-being. We know that if we do it right and proper in the early years, children will thrive throughout their school years and adult lives.

Childhood is influenced by both nature and nurture (genes and environment). The quality of a child's early settings, as well as the availability of relevant experiences at the appropriate developmental time, are important factors in how each child's brain architecture develops.

The emotional, social, and physical development of children has a direct impact on their total development and on who they will become as adults. It is critical to recognize the importance of investing in children (beginning at a young age) in order to enhance their future well-being.

Meaning of Child Development

Child development is a specialized area of study which concerns itself the growth and development of a child right from the moment of conception to adolescence.

The term development means a progressive series of changes that occurs as a result of maturation and learning development implies qualitative changes. This means that development does not consist of adding inches to one's height or increasing kg in weight. These include changes in abilities like learning to speak, changes in behavior, interests, comprehension, etc.

According to Laura Berk, Child development is a field of study devoted to understanding human constancy and change from conception through adolescence.

Scope of Child Development

In your child's growth, especially in the early years, a well-balanced concentration on learning is critical. Child ventures' curriculum is made up of aspects from three different educational methods: Montessori, High Scope, and Core Knowledge. Each teaching style benefits your child's learning in a different way.

High Scope is a hands-on method that fosters active learning beginning in infancy and going throughout toddlerhood.

Here are eight ways the High Scope learning technique fosters child development for your little one, including abilities such as music, movement, numbers, and time:

Emphasizes Problem Solving skills: The High Scope technique emphasizes social and emotional development, which are important life skills for your child. Teachers encourage youngsters to carry out conflict resolution processes independently by addressing issues through a sequence of steps.

Encouraged Use of All Senses: High Scope activities differ depending on the group, age level, and school setting. Most activities include engaging several senses at once, with active, hands-on learning being the main proponent of High Scope activities.

Education Through Movement: Children have a natural need to move, sing, and play throughout their early years. This fact is used by High Scope to incorporate developmentally appropriate activities into its teaching methods.

Fosters Decision-Making Skills: Children in the High Scope programmed to have the freedom to pick what they want to do and how they want to learn on a daily basis.

Promotes Independence: Children's independence grows as they have the opportunity to strengthen decision-making abilities by selecting their own activities. They become less reliant on teachers to educate them during the day and instead search for answers.

Cultivates Curiosity: Children are encouraged to further investigate what hobbies interest them, similar to developing independence, with the guidance of their teachers. For example, if a child expresses an interest in mixing paint colors to produce new shades, the instructor will assist this activity by gathering resources.

Increases Confidence: The High Scope technique is designed to work for all pupils, regardless of their background or aptitude. Children build on their own abilities to design a learning path that suits and supports their particular learning interests.

Creates Social Relations: Interactions in a group setting, including small and big group experiences and activities, create crucial communication and social skills.

The High Scope technique has been integrated into the curriculum for the Infant and Toddler programmed at Child ventures. To learn more about the curriculum, please contact us.

Difference between Growth and Development

What is Growth? An increase in the size of an object or a live creature is referred to as growth. It's been used in phrases like "the lump has expanded in size." The term "growth" refers to the act of growing. As an example, 'the country's economy grew rapidly.' It denotes a rise in the worth of something. 'The number of hospitals in the city has increased.' Growth can refer to a rise in the size of a crop or the production of a particular fruit. 'The farmer was astounded by the incredible grape growth.'

The term "full growth" is used to describe a mature state. 'The investment has reached its full potential.' Any industry that is rapidly developing can be labeled as a "growth industry." The phrase 'steel industry is currently the growth industry' is an example of its application. A 'growth stock,' on the other hand, is one that tends to increase in capital value. This particular application is common in the stock market.

What is development? The term "development" refers to a rise in one's degree of functioning. It's been used in phrases like "he evolved into a nice cop." The term "development" can refer to an improvement in one's health. As an example, 'he now has a better pulse rate.'

The term "development" is used to describe the process of being developed or the act of developing. In fact, it is employed to communicate the concept of a "development stage." In a nutshell, the term "growth" can be considered a subset of the term "development." One of the clearest examples of its application is the phrase "the lump grew into a tumor due to an increase in its growth." The phrase "an increase in its growth" in this case denoted an increase in the lump's size. As a result, the term "growth" might be considered a subset of "development."

The term "development" can refer to a steady shift. The word "development" can be used to describe a development process. You may use something like, "the process of developing an image." A fully developed state or piece of land is an example of development. 'A developed portion of agricultural land,' 'a developed region of land,' and similar expressions are instances of this type of usage. The former word refers to fertility, but the latter phrase refers to an improvement in living conditions.

A 'development area' is an area where new industries are fostered in order to create jobs and stimulate the economy. The related use is: 'This country abounds in numerous development areas.' Take note of the phrase "the boy has matured into a lovely youth." This sentence alludes to the growth of his body's features. As a result, the meanings of the two words 'growth' and 'development' are vastly different.

Difference between Growth and Development

Growth is the process of something growing larger, longer, more numerous, or more important, which is usually a physical change; development is the process of something changing (usually for the better) into a new stage or improving, which can be physical, social, or psychological.

An increase in the size of an object or a live creature is referred to as growth. The term "development" refers to a rise in one's degree of functioning.

The term "growth" refers to the act of growing. It denotes a rise in the worth of something. Growth can refer to a rise in the size of a crop or the production of a particular fruit.

The term "development" can refer to an improvement in one's health. The term "development" can refer to a steady shift.

Interdisciplinary Basis of child development

Typically demanding a spark of creativity coupled with experimentation,

Interdisciplinary teaching can be an ambitious approach to use in your classroom.

Fortunately, there are activities you can implement relatively easily that deliver research-backed benefits. These include:

- Improved Critical Thinking — Students should improve their analysis abilities by using approaches from different disciplines.
- Better Bias Recognition — To solve a problem that demands an interdisciplinary approach, students must typically use information rooted in a range of perspectives. This can often challenge their pre-existing ideas to help them identify bias in themselves in others.
- Preparation for Future Problems — Using skills and knowledge from different disciplines is practice for solving problems outside school walls.

Framed by a definition and supplemented with unit design steps, below are 10 interdisciplinary teaching activities and examples. To choose ones that suit your schedule, they're categorized by length.

A Multidisciplinary Approach to Early Childhood Education and Care examines early childhood education and care in Australia from a variety of angles, emphasizing the field's complexity and the necessity for a truly interdisciplinary approach. It claims that only a comprehensive understanding of each viewpoint would allow for a clear future for early childhood education in Australia, and that all political parties should work together to improve policy and provision to assure the sector's support and development.

By exploring current government policies, as well as individual and communal initiatives, the chapters provide insights into how children and families are positioned in educational change. Positive, behavioral, developmental, economic, sociocultural, and postmodern models are among the paradigms studied. Garvis and Manning identify field issues and suggest modifications to assist establish an interdisciplinary approach to help decrease the educational outcomes disadvantage gap.

This book is supposed to stimulate considerable advances in early childhood education and care in Australia, with recommendations addressed at stakeholders from several disciplines. This book will stimulate new ways of thinking about policy and provision development for the future by providing crucial insights into the landscape of early childhood education and care.

From birth until age five, there are many opportunities and risks for healthy physical, emotional, social, and cognitive development

Human development is the consequence of a complicated interaction between genetic predispositions and environmental factors. Nature and nurture, both separately and in combination, play important roles throughout a person's existence. In particular, the first few years of life are a critical time throughout the development process, setting the groundwork for cognitive functioning, behavioral, social, and self-regulatory capacities, and physical health in childhood and beyond.

A lot of elements are important for optimal growth throughout these early years. They include the nature of early caregiver connections, the level of cognitive stimulation provided, and availability to proper nourishment and health care. Some children will be robust in the face of early childhood stressors, while others' healthy development will be jeopardized, with temporary or long-term consequences.

In the years leading up to school admission, a significant number of youngsters are exposed to dangers that may restrict their development

Living in poverty, being a single parent, and having a woman with less than a high school degree, among other factors, all increase the risk of developmental delay. Nearly half of a recent cohort of kindergarten students in the United States studied as part of the US Department of Education's Early Childhood Longitudinal Study of the Kindergarten Class of 1998–1999 (ECLS-K) experienced one or more of our risk factors. Nearly one in every six people was subjected to more than one type of abuse. Exposure to such dangers does not always result in developmental issues. Some youngsters are resilient, but the consequences for others can be severe.

Disparities in school preparedness result from differences in early childhood experiences, and these inequalities frequently endure

Early childhood disadvantages have ramifications for how prepared children are when they start school. School preparation includes not only cognitive abilities, but also those related to socializing, self-control, and learning styles.

While these readiness indicators suggest that children who grow up in more enriched surroundings are better prepared for school, longitudinal data show that these early gaps continue and even enlarge as children advance through school. As a result, achievement inequalities tend to increase over time as disadvantaged students do not progress at the same rate as their more advantaged peers.

Children from disadvantaged homes are also more likely to get special education, repeat grades, and drop out of high school. Lower levels of school achievement are linked to adverse life outcomes in later years. Low employment rates, welfare dependency, and delinquency and crime are examples of the latter. Even if only a part of these negative childhood and adult outcomes can be avoided, the advantages could be significant.

Early childhood interventions are intended to help children cope with a variety of stressors while also promoting healthy growth

Early childhood interventions are intended to act as a buffer against the many risk factors that may jeopardize a child's healthy development in the years leading up to school enrollment. While they all have the same goal, early childhood interventions use a wide range of approaches; there is no one-size-fits-all approach. Programs differ in terms of the results they seek to achieve and the risk factors they examine when determining eligibility, such as poor socioeconomic position and single parenthood.

They differ in terms of whether they are directed at the child, the parent, or both, as well as the level of personalized attention they provide. Different programmers cater to children of all ages and differ in terms of the services they provide, where they are provided, and how many hours per week they are provided.

Early childhood therapies that are rigorously evaluated can help us understand what outcomes they may enhance

Although we may anticipate positive outcomes from early childhood programmers, a scientifically solid review is essential to determine whether they deliver on their promise. Because of the wide range of early childhood intervention approaches, such evaluations are required across the entire spectrum of program models, ideally with the ability to determine the effects of changing key program characteristics.

While numerous early childhood interventions have been adopted and some have been evaluated in some way, only a small percentage have been evaluated using scientifically sound methodologies. We found published evaluations for 20 early childhood programs with well-implemented experimental designs or strong quasi-experimental designs after researching the literature on studies of early childhood interventions that matched our criteria for rigorous assessment.

Some initiatives were omitted from the list because their evaluations did not fulfil minimal scientific rigor standards (e.g., a large enough sample size). Sixteen programs had the most evidence since they tracked results from kindergarten admission to graduation.

Stages of Development

Prenatal Development

How did you become the person you are today? Your prenatal development took place in an ordered and delicate sequence, beginning as a single cell structure and ending with your birth.

Prenatal development is divided into three stages: germinal, embryonic, and fetal. Let's take a look at what the developing infant goes through at each of these stages.

Germinal Stage (Weeks 1- 2)

You learned about genetics and DNA during the earlier topic of biopsychology in the book. At the moment of conception, the DNA of the mother and father is passed on to the kid. When sperm fertilizes an egg and generates a zygote, it is called conception. When sperm and egg combine, a zygote is formed as a one-cell structure. At this phase, the baby's genetic makeup and sex are determined. The zygote divides and multiplies during the first week following conception, going from a one-cell structure to two cells, four cells, eight cells, and so on. Mitosis is the name given to the process of cell division.

Mitosis is a delicate process, with only about half of all zygotes surviving past the first two weeks (Hall, 2004). There are 100 cells after 5 days of mitosis, and billions of cells after 9 months. As cells divide, they become more specialized, resulting in the formation of various organs and body components. The mass of cells has not yet attached themselves to the lining of the mother's uterus in the germinal stage. The following stage begins after that.

Embryonic Stage (Weeks 3- 8)

The zygote goes down the fallopian tubes and inserts itself in the uterine lining after dividing for 7–10 days and having 150 cells. This multicellular organism is referred to as an embryo once it has been implanted. The placenta is now formed by the growth of blood vessels. The placenta is a uterine structure that transports nutrients and oxygen from the mother to the developing embryo via the umbilical cord.

The embryo's basic structures begin to form the sections that will become the head, chest, and abdomen. The heart begins to beat and organs build and function during the embryonic stage. The neural tube develops into the spinal cord and brain along the back of the embryo.

Fetal Stage (Weeks 9- 40)

The embryo is known as a fetus when it is about nine weeks old. The fetus is approximately the size of a kidney bean at this point, and it's starting to take on the shape of a human being when the "tail" fades away.

The sex organs begin to distinguish between 9 and 12 weeks. The fetus is around 4.5 inches long at 16 weeks. Fingers and toes are fully formed, with visible fingerprints. The fetus can weigh up to 1.4 pounds by the time it reaches the sixth month of development (24 weeks). The fetus' hearing has matured to the point that it can respond to sounds. Internal organs such as the lungs, heart, stomach, and intestines have matured to the degree where a prematurely born fetus can survive outside the mother's womb.

The brain continues to grow and develop throughout the prenatal stage, approximately doubling in size from weeks 16 to 28. The fetus is almost ready to be born at 36 weeks. By week 37, all of the fetus' organ systems have developed to the point where it may survive outside the mother's uterus without many of the hazards associated with preterm birth. Until the fetus reaches 40 weeks, it continues to acquire weight and length. The fetus has very little room to move around by this time, and birth is imminent.

Influences During Pregnancy

Genetic and environmental factors can influence development at each prenatal stage. The developing fetus is totally reliant on the mother for survival. It is critical that the mother takes care of herself and receives prenatal care, which is medical care provided during pregnancy that monitors both the mother and the fetus's health.

From Infancy to Childhood

A newborn weighs about 7.5 pounds on average. A newborn, despite his small size, is not completely helpless because his reflexes and sensory abilities enable him to interact with his surroundings from birth. Every healthy baby is born with newborn reflexes, which are inborn automatic responses to specific types of stimulation. Reflexes help the newborn survive until it is able to perform more complex behaviors—these reflexes are critical for survival. They appear in babies whose brains are developing normally and usually disappear around the age of 4–5 months. Let's look at a few of these newborn reflexes. The rooting reflex is the newborn's reaction to anything that moves. When you stroke a baby's cheek, she naturally turns her head in that direction and starts sucking. The sucking reflex refers to the automatic, unlearned sucking motions performed by infants with their mouths. Several other fascinating newborn reflexes can be seen. For example, if you insert your finger into a newborn's hand, you will observe the grasping reflex, in which a baby automatically grasps anything that comes into contact with his palms. The Moro reflex is the newborn's reaction when she feels she is about to fall. The baby spreads her arms, then pulls them in, and (usually) cries. How do you believe these reflexes aid in survival during the first few months of life?

Physical Growth and Development

The physical development of the body is rapid during infancy, toddlerhood, and early childhood ([link]). Newborns weigh between 5 and 10 pounds on average, and their weight doubles in six months and triples in a year. Weight will have quadrupled by the age of two, so a two-year-old should weigh between 20 and 40 pounds. A newborn's average length is 19.5 inches, increasing to 29.5 inches at 12 months and 34.4 inches at 2 years old (WHO Multicentre Growth Reference Study Group, 2006).

Motor development occurs in an orderly sequence as infants move from reflexive reactions (e.g., sucking and rooting) to more advanced motor functioning. For instance, babies first learn to hold their heads up, then to sit with assistance, and then to sit unassisted, followed later by crawling and then walking.

Our ability to move our bodies and manipulate objects is referred to as Motor Skills. Fine motor skills are the muscles in our fingers, toes, and eyes that allow us to coordinate small actions (e.g., grasping a toy, writing with a pencil, and using a spoon). Gross motor skills are concerned with large muscle groups that control our arms and legs, as well as larger movements (e.g., balancing, running, and jumping).

Development of the Mind(Cognitive Development)

Young children exhibit significant development of their cognitive abilities in addition to rapid physical growth. Piaget believed that children's ability to understand objects, such as learning that a rattle makes a noise when shaken, is a cognitive skill that develops gradually as a child grows and interacts with his or her environment. Today, developmental psychologists believe Piaget was mistaken. Researchers discovered that even very young children understand objects and how they work long before they have any experience with them (Baillargeon, 1987; Baillargeon, Li, Gertner, & Wu, 2011).

There are cognitive milestones that we expect children to reach, just as there are physical milestones. It is beneficial to be aware of these developmental milestones as children develop new abilities to think, problem-solve, and communicate. For example, around 6–9 months, infants shake their heads "no," and around 9–12 months, they respond to verbal requests to do things like "wave bye-bye" or "blow a kiss." Remember Piaget's theories on object permanence? We can expect children to understand that objects continue to exist even when they are not visible by the age of 8 months. Toddlers (those aged 12–24 months) enjoy games like hiding and seek because they have mastered object permanence which recognizes that when someone leaves the room, they will return (Loop, 2013). When asked to find objects, toddlers will point to pictures in books and look at inappropriate places.

At this age, children undergo a significant cognitive change. Remember that Piaget labeled 2–3-year-olds as egocentric, which means they are unaware of the perspectives of others. Children between the ages of 3 and 5 begin to understand that other people have thoughts, feelings, and beliefs that differ from their own. This is referred to as theory-of-mind (TOM).

Attachment

Children's psychosocial development occurs as they form relationships, interact with others, and learn to understand and manage their emotions. Forming healthy attachments is a major social milestone of infancy in terms of social and emotional development. Attachment is a long-term connection or bond with another person. Developmental psychologists are curious about how infants achieve this milestone. They inquire, for example, "How do parent-infant attachment bonds form?" What effect does neglect have on these bonds? What factors contribute to children's attachment differences?

Self-Concept

The development of a positive sense of self is the primary psychosocial milestone of childhood, just as attachment is the primary psychosocial milestone of infancy. What factors influence the development of self-awareness? Infants lack a self-concept, or understanding of who they are. If you put a baby in front of a mirror, she will reach out to touch her reflection, believing it is another baby. A toddler, on the other hand, will recognize herself in the mirror by the age of 18 months. What evidence do we have?

In a well-known experiment, a researcher painted a red dot on the noses of children before placing them in front of a mirror (Amsterdam, 1972).

The formation of a positive self-concept is essential for healthy development. Children who have a positive self-concept are more confident, perform better in school, act independently, and are more willing to try new things (Maccoby, 1980; Ferrer & Fugate, 2003). The development of a positive self-concept begins in Erikson's toddlerhood stage when children gain autonomy and confidence in their abilities. When children compare themselves to others in elementary school, they continue to develop their self-concept.

Stages of Adolescence

Adolescence is the time when a person transitions from childhood to adulthood. It involves significant physical and psychological changes in a young person's life. Both children and their families may experience excitement and worry as a result of the numerous physical, sexual, cognitive, social, and emotional changes that occur during this period. Understanding what to expect at different stages of adolescence and early adulthood might help to encourage healthy development.

Early adolescence (Ages 10 to 13)

Children often begin to grow faster at this age. They also start to notice other physical changes, such as hair growth under the arms and near the genitals, female breast development, and male testicular enlargement. They typically begin a year or two earlier in girls than in boys, and some changes can occur as early as age 8 in females and age 9 in males. Many girls begin their periods at the age of twelve, about two to three years after the onset of breast growth.

Some people may be both curious and anxious about these changes in their bodies, especially if they are unsure of what to anticipate or what is normal. At this age, some children may begin to question their gender identity, and puberty can be a challenging time for transgender youngsters.

Early teenage thought is definite and black-and-white. Without many areas in between, things are either right or bad, amazing or dreadful. It's natural for young people to focus their thoughts on themselves at this age (called "egocentrism"). As a result, preteens and early adolescent girls and boys are frequently self-conscious about their appearance and believe that they are constantly being scrutinized by their classmates.

Pre-teens have a stronger desire for seclusion. They may begin to look for ways to be self-sufficient from their family. They may push boundaries during this process, and if parents or guardians reinforce restrictions, they may react violently.

Middle Adolescence (Ages 14 to 17)

During middle adolescence, physical changes from puberty continue. The majority of males will have begun their growth spurt, and puberty-related changes will be ongoing. As their voices fall, they may experience some vocal cracking. Acne affects some people. Females' physical transformations may be practically complete, and most girls now have regular periods.

Many teenagers grow interested in romantic and sexual relationships at this age. They may doubt and explore their sexual identity, which can be difficult if they do not have peer, family, or community support. Self-stimulation, often known as masturbation, is another common approach for the youth of all genders to explore sex and sexuality.

As they strive for more independence, many middle teens have more disagreements with their parents. They may spend more time with friends and less time with relatives. They are particularly conscious of their appearance, and peer pressure is likely to be at its greatest at this age.

In this period, the brain continues to evolve and mature, but there are still numerous distinctions between how a normal middle adolescent thinks and how an adult thinks. Much of this is due to the fact that the frontal lobes are the last portions of the brain to mature, and development does not end until well into one's twenties! The frontal lobes are important for complicated decision-making, impulse control, and the ability to weigh various options and consequences. Middle teenagers are better at thinking abstractly and considering "the big picture," but they may still be unable to apply it in the present.

Late Adolescence (Age 18- 21 and beyond):

Late teenagers have reached the full adult height and have completed their physical development. By this time, they should have more impulse control and be able to accurately assess risks and rewards. Teenagers approaching early adulthood have a deeper sense of self-identity and are able to identify their own ideals. They may become more future-oriented, making judgments based on their ambitions and beliefs. Friendships and romantic relationships become more stable as a result of these changes.

They grow emotionally and physically estranged from their loved ones. Many people, on the other hand, re-establish an "adult" relationship with their parents, seeing them as more of a peer with whom to seek advice and discuss mature issues rather than an authority figure.

Domains of Development

Living and learning go hand in hand from birth to death. Nothing, however, compares to our first few years of life, when we learn to walk, talk, and interact with other people and our surroundings, as well as process how these activities make us feel. Although children develop at varying speeds, there are a number of crucial developmental milestones that each individual should achieve.

Early intervention treatments can be used to try to minimize or limit the impact of a suspected intellectual or developmental handicap once a defect has been identified.

A child must either obtain a qualifying diagnosis (such as autism) or show a 25% or greater delay in one or more of the five categories of development to be eligible for early intervention. Physical, cognitive, linguistic, socio-emotional, and adaptive abilities are among them. Let's look at each of these areas to see what they entail and what to look for.

Physical: A child must either obtain a qualifying diagnosis (such as autism) or show a 25% or greater delay in one or more of the five categories of development to be eligible for early intervention. Physical, cognitive, linguistic, socio-emotional, and adaptive abilities are among them. Let's look at each of these areas to see what they entail and what to look for.

Humans acquire physical ability in three directions: top to bottom, center to the periphery, and center to the periphery. As a baby grows older, he or she will be able to swivel their head and sit upright, before reaching, grabbing, and finally walking and running (2-3 years). During this time, the infant should be able to respond and react spontaneously to stimuli in his or her physical environment.

Cognitive: The ability to mentally digest information - to think, reason, and understand what's going on around you — falls under the cognitive domain of development. Jean Piaget, a developmental psychologist, separated cognitive development into four stages.

Humans are primarily limited to seeing the world on a sensory level throughout the sensorimotor stage of cognitive development (0-2 years). And the grownup makes a wry expression at you? Make a fool of yourself by laughing at what you see. Is there a toy dangling in front of you? Make a grab for it.

When a child reaches the preoperational stage (2-6 years), he or she begins to employ language in their study of people and their surroundings.

In most situations, though, logical functioning isn't quite there yet, and the youngster may struggle to "put it all together."

Prior to puberty, a kid should have reached the concrete operational stage (7-11 years), at which point he or she can comprehend events and information at face value but cannot handle abstracts or hypotheticals.

People aged 12 and up are said to be in the formal operational stage, capable of performing the complex mental gymnastics that distinguish humans. Abstract thinking, such as imagining hypothetical scenarios, formulating plans, and sorting through various points of view, becomes a regular aspect of dealing with reality.

Communicative: Understanding, utilizing, and manipulating language may be the single most powerful skill a person can acquire. Phonology (the formation of a language's constituent sounds into words), syntax (the fitting of those words together into sentences according to a language's rules and conventions), semantics (meaning and shades of meaning), and pragmatics (the use of language) are the four aspects of language development (how the language is applied in practical and interpersonal communication). Individuals' verbal communication skills vary greatly, but by the age of two, many toddlers are capable of at least telegraphic speech, which consists of brief words that communicate the core of a wish or need.

Socioemotional: To truly thrive, we must learn to interact with others and exist happily inside ourselves. As a child matures in the socioemotional realm, he or she learns to successfully manage his or her own internal emotional state as well as interpret others' social signs. Strong emotions can be properly controlled or communicated; confrontations may be handled without resorting to violence, and we can learn to empathize with others.

A baby should be reacting to facial expressions and reciprocating by the age of six months.

By a year, obvious preferences in terms of likes and dislikes, as well as recognition of the familiar vs the unknown, should have emerged.

A kid should be participating in parallel play with his or her peers by the age of two. Even though each child is engaged in a different activity, they are interested in and comfortable in each other's company.

By three years, self-awareness and the ability to communicate sentiments should have developed.

The child should be able to work cooperatively with others, follow simple rules, and manage emotions without tantrums or aggressiveness by the age of four.

Adaptive: Adaptive development refers to the aspect of growing up that involves self-care, such as eating, drinking, toileting, bathing, and dressing oneself. It also requires being aware of one's surroundings and any potential threats, as well as keeping oneself safe and secure. Before his or her fourth birthday, a kid should have made significant growth in these areas.

Role of Heredity, Environment, Maturation, and Learning in Children's Development

Role of Heredity and Development:

Meaning of Heredity:

Each person has a unique set of actions and personality traits. The influence of heredity and environment is visible in this disparity. Indeed, heredity and environment play a significant effect in the development of a person's personality and other characteristics.

Without heredity, no one can be born, and genes cannot grow properly without the right environment. From the moment of conception, an individual's heredity is there, and some external conditions begin to influence him at this period as well.

An individual's heredity is determined by his parents' genes, which means that whatever one contributes to his children is passed down through the genes. The mechanism of heredity is detailed in the following section:

Mechanism of Heredity:

Mating: The first step in reproduction is mating. The zygote is the outcome of the combination of male sperm and female ovum.

Growth: The fertilized cell or zygote is divided several times.

chromosomes: Every woman and male inherit 23 chromosomes from each parent, for a total of 46 chromosomes.

Genes: Each chromosome is made up of microscopic particles called genes that range in size from 40 to 100.

Chance Factor: Both the ovum and the sperm have 23 pairs of chromosomes before fertilization. The genes in the sperm's chromosomes pair with the genes in the ovum during conception, determining the offspring's potential characteristics and qualities.

Meaning of Environment

The term "environment" refers to the whole of a person's surroundings in which he or she must live. An individual's environment is psychologically linked to all of the stimuli he encounters from conception to death. Natural and social environments are the two main types of environments. All of the things and forces on and around the earth that influence a person are referred to as the natural environment.

We mean the environment that a person perceives around him when he first becomes aware of society, such as language, religion, custom, tradition, means of communication, means of luxury, family, school, social groups, and so on.

Educational Implications of Heredity and Environment

Human development is greatly influenced by knowledge of heredity and the environment. Human growth is influenced by both genes and the surrounding environment. Children's growth patterns are influenced by both inheritance and environment.

The educational pattern, methods, and learning environment should be created by the instructor in the teaching-learning scenario based on the developmental pattern of the children. As a result, understanding heredity and environment benefit the teacher in a variety of ways, which are addressed further below.

Knowledge of genetics and the environment aids the teacher in understanding the children's various needs and talents.

It assists him in providing suitable educational, vocational, and personal direction to his children.

It aids the teacher in classifying children as talented, average, or slow learners and assigning them to different types of schooling.

It aids the teacher in creating a more conducive learning atmosphere in the classroom.

It aids the instructor in understanding the idea of individual variations and arranging the educational experience appropriately.

Role of Maturation and Learning in Children's Life

By their very nature, all living things or organisms go through a maturing process. Humans are special in that while they age, they also go through the process of learning through cognition, making maturation and learning intertwined. So, what exactly is maturation? What exactly is learning? What function does maturation play in learning if they are intertwined?

A newborn baby is the world's most helpless creature. His head is far too big for his body. His legs and feet are too small for him. He is unable to stand or even hold his head up. His hands are unsuitable for any skill. He doesn't have any teeth. His voice is audible, but it is monotonous for human speech. He has eyes and ears, but he never uses them. He sleeps the majority of the time. Despite his large head, his brain appears to be inactive.

The baby, on the other hand, is capable of development. He possesses the ability to grow. His legs and hands grow to the length of a human being. His muscles develop to the size and strength required for standing, walking, and running. His teeth were already present in rudimentary form.

At the appropriate ages, his form will grow, harden, and breakthrough his gums. His mouth and larynx develop into adaptable speech organs. His brain will not only grow in size but also in the fineness of its microscopic structure, allowing it to participate in a variety of human activities. The transition of an organism from an immature to a mature state is referred to as maturation.

If it were possible to accelerate a child's development and have it completed in a single week, would that week-old grown-up be a true adult, a competent adult? It would be impossible for him to learn much about the world in a week, let alone master the language and the thousands of skilful acts that adults are expected to perform. For this, we must add to the power of growth another important capacity which may be called the power of learning.

Learning: Learning, according to William Huitt, is the generally permanent change in an individual's conduct or potential behavior as a result of practice experience. Learning, according to Schunk, is a long-term change in behavior or the capacity to behave in a certain way that occurs as a result of practice or other forms of experience. We can draw from these definitions that three factors are present in learning: change, persistence, and the result of experience or practice.

These are the three events that makeup learning. Change, Endurance across time, and Consequence of Experience is, in fact, Schunk's three core requirements for what constitutes learning. Learning, in my opinion, is a process that begins with the learner acquiring stimuli from his or her environment, whether through experience or instruction, and culminates in a lasting change in the learner's behavior, abilities, or wisdom through cognition or mental processes. This adjustment must be long-lasting; else, there will be no learning.

Maturation: Unlike maturity, which is the outcome of biological growth and development, learning (Huitt) is a psychological process. Maturation is a natural process that occurs without human involvement. Learning occurs when a person's intellect interacts with his physical and social environment. Maturation and learning, on the other hand, are linked. As a person ages, so does his or her knowledge, talents, and attitude. A youngster learns only the most fundamental things, but as he grows older, his knowledge expands, allowing him to learn more complex things. It is critical that teachers keep this link in mind.

Teachers must understand the learner's maturity and psychological capability in order to establish learning strategies and materials that are appropriate for the learner's maturity level. The students in the classroom have varying levels of maturity and ability. If the lessons given are beyond a child's age range, he or she will be disappointed. On the other hand, if insufficient is provided, the opportunity to develop a child's potential is squandered. The attention span of children is one example. Children have a limited attention span, and if this isn't factored into the teacher's teaching technique, a lot of the teachings will be wasted.

Thus, we can say that Learning is critical for acquiring new knowledge, skills, and attitudes required for a successful life. Growing and learning are equally important. According to Woodworth and Marquis, "while many animals reach maturity in a few weeks or months after birth, the human being takes about 18 years, and during all of these years he is learning." What he is as an adult is determined by how well he has matured and what he has learned."

Maturation and learning go hand in hand in the process of human development; the growth of the structures of the body allows for the performance of various activities, and these activities allow for the performance of learning. The majority of the abilities of the adult are, "therefore, dependent on both maturation and learning. There are some abilities that do not depend on learning.

Piaget's theory of development: -

The theory of cognitive development developed by French scientist Jean Piaget (1896–1980) is the most well-known and influential. Piaget's hypothesis, initially published in 1952, was based on decades of detailed observation of children in their natural circumstances, including his own, as opposed to behaviorists' laboratory trials. Piaget was concerned in how children reacted to their surroundings, but he proposed a more active role for them than learning theory predicted. He saw a child's knowledge as being made up of schemas, which he defined as "fundamental units of knowledge used to organize past experiences and provide a foundation for understanding future ones."

Assimilation and accommodation, two complimentary processes identified by Piaget, are constantly changing schemas. Assimilation is the process of assimilating new data by incorporating it into an existing schema. To put it another way, humans assimilate new experiences by linking them to previous experiences. Accommodation, on the other hand, occurs when the schema itself changes to accommodate new information. Piaget defined cognitive development as a constant effort to achieve equilibration, which he defined as a balance between assimilation and accommodation.

Infancy: -

Infants learn to utilize their senses to investigate the world around them as soon as they are born. Most babies can focus on and follow moving objects, recognize pitch and loudness of sound, see all colors and discern hue and brightness, and begin anticipating events such as sucking at the sight of a nipple. Infants can remember faces, reproduce facial emotions such as smiling and frowning, and respond to familiar sounds by the age of three months.

Babies are just six months old when they begin to comprehend how the world works. They copy sounds, like hearing their own voice, recognize their parents, avoid strangers, distinguish between animate and inanimate objects, and measure distance based on object size. They also understand that if they drop an object, they can retrieve it. Babies can recognize their names between the ages of four and seven months.

Toddlerhood: -

Toddlers have achieved the "sensorimotor" stage of Piaget's theory of cognitive development, which involves rudimentary reasoning, between the ages of 18 months and three years. For example, they can recognize the permanence of items and people, follow the displacement of objects visually, and use instruments and equipment. Toddlers begin to seek greater independence, which can provide difficulties for parents concerned about their children's safety. They also comprehend discipline and what constitutes appropriate and inappropriate behavior, as well as the meanings of phrases such as "please" and "thank you."

Preschool: -

Preschoolers, ages three to six, should be in Piaget's cognitive development theory's "preoperational" stage, which means they are using their imagery and memory skills. They should be taught to study and memories, and their worldview is typically quite self-centered. Preschoolers have often developed social interaction abilities, such as playing and cooperating with other kids their age. It's typical for preschoolers to push their cognitive capacities to their limits, and they pick up on bad concepts and behaviors like talking back to adults, lying, and bullying. Preschoolers' cognitive development also includes increasing their attention span, learning to read, and forming disciplined routines, such as doing housework.

School age: -

Younger school-age children, ages six to twelve, should be at the "concrete operations" stage of Piaget's cognitive development theory, which is characterized by the ability to think and solve problems through logical and coherent actions. They grasp the principles of permanence and conservation by understanding that despite changes in external appearance, volume, weight, and numbers can remain constant. These kids should be able to draw on their previous experiences to explain why certain things happen. Their attention span should improve as they become older, going from about 15 minutes at age six to an hour at age nine.

Adolescents between the ages of 12 and 18 should be in Piaget's "formal operations" stage of cognitive development. It is characterized by a greater ability to think through problems and circumstances on one's own. Pure abstractions, such as philosophy and higher math concepts, should be understandable to adolescents. Children should be able to learn and use general information to adapt to specific situations at this age. They should also be able to learn the specialized knowledge and abilities required for a particular job. A cognitive transition is an important part of the adolescent experience. Adolescents think in ways that are more mature, efficient, and complex than children's thinking. There are five ways to look at this talent.

Principles of Growth & Development and their Educational Implication

Introduction: -

Concepts are assessed through state exams and Common Core Assessments. The principal idea of the question, for example, is used in the 5th grade Smarter Balanced Assessment. Students will need to understand the essential notion in order to choose the correct answer.

Meaning of Growth: -

State tests and Common Core Assessments are used to evaluate concepts. In the 5th grade Smarter Balanced Assessment, for example, the question's main premise is employed. In order to choose the proper answer, students must first grasp the fundamental concept.

Definition: -

Arnold Gessel claims that "Rather than the environment, growth is a function of the organism. The environment provides the soil and surroundings for development manifestations, but these manifestations are the result of an inherent, inner organism and an intrinsic development physiology. Growth is such a complex and delicate process that it necessitates strong stabilising mechanisms, as well as an inherent balance in the overall pattern and direction of the growth trend."

Meaning of Development: -

Overall changes in shape, form, or structure are referred to as development. Development is a lifelong and ongoing process. It begins with the birth of a kid and concludes with the individual's death. The term "development" refers to the changes that occur in an organism as a whole, rather than the changes that occur in individual sections.

Definition: -

Development psychology is concerned with the study of behavioural changes across time. It refers to a process in which a person's growth and capabilities vary throughout time as a result of maturation and interaction with the environment.

Principles of Growth and Development: -

Principle of community:

Community development is a result of community development. It never stops from the womb to the tomb. Every person develops his or her body and mind from the moment he or she is born.

Principle of Individual differences:

Individual variations in development are unaffected. Each youngster develops at his or her own pace.

Principle of orderly development:

The process of development progresses from broad to specific. The youngster first learns general information before moving on to detailed or specific information.

Uniformity of pattern:

Although development does not occur at the same rate for everyone and differs significantly from one person to the next, it does follow a predictable pattern.

Principle of interaction and maturation and learning:

Maturation and learning both contribute to growth and development. Maturation refers to changes in a developing organism, whereas learning refers to behavioural changes.

Principle of unique development:

Individuals differ in terms of their time patterns, e.g., all children start sitting up, crawling, and standing up at the same time.

Principle of differential development:

There is a principle that male and female children develop differently. In comparison to boys, girls mature earlier.

Principle of inter- related development:

The process of development is holistic. His physical, intellectual, emotional, social, and other types of growth are all intertwined and dependent on one another.

Educational Implication

For parents, instructors, and educators, understanding the principles of growth and development is extremely important and beneficial. The following are some examples of how growth and development principles might be applied: -

Adjusting school program: -

It assists the instructor in adapting the school programme, procedures, and practices to the child's level of development, allowing him to become more productive in the classroom.

Sympathetic Handling: -

It assists parents and teachers in treating their children or students sympathetically and realistically solving their difficulties.

Effective guidance: -

It assists the instructor in treating the right guidance programme by allowing the teacher to grasp the individual differences of the pupils.

Importance of childhood period: -

It assists parents and teachers in comprehending the significance of the childhood era. As a result, parents and instructors should provide a wide range of social and emotional experiences for their children.

Right expectation: -

Its knowledge enables us to anticipate what to expect from an individual child in terms of physical, mental, and social development at various phases of development.

Importance of environment: -

It aids parents and teachers in understanding and instilling the value of heredity and a healthy environment, as well as assisting us in paying proper attention to environmental conditions.

Characteristics of Development

The following are some of the most essential development characteristics:

Development as a continuous process: -

The process of growth and development begins at conception and continues until the individual reaches adulthood. It progresses at a steady but steady pace rather than in leaps and bounds. Both physical and mental features develop progressively until they achieve their ultimate potential.

Development proceeds from general to specific response: -

To begin with, a child's response or reactions are of a generic type. He uses his entire body to react to the circumstance and external inputs. He gradually develops distinct answers. This is true not only of his bodily responses, but also of his cognitive and emotional responses. A child's reactions, which are initially general in character, later become more specific. This is an indication of maturation and growth.

The development follows a pattern: -

Development takes place in a systematic and sequential manner. Thus, the sequence of human development is infancy, early childhood, later childhood, adolescence, and adulthood.

A different aspect of growth develops at different stages: -

Despite the fact that development is a continual process, the rate of growth is not consistent. As a result, there are times of rapid growth and periods of slow growth. The pace of growth slows throughout the first three years of life, but accelerates again during the adolescent stage. Similarly, not all areas of the body grow at the same rate, and not all aspects of mental development evolve at the same rate. As a result, they mature at various times.

Most traits are correlated in development: -

In general, it has been assumed that a child with above-average intellectual development is also exceptional in many other areas, such as health, sociability, and unique aptitudes. Similarly, his mental development is intertwined with his physical development.

Development is a product of the interaction of the organism and environment: -

Neither genes nor the environment alone is responsible for an individual's development. Both are responsible for human growth and development, while it is impossible to say exactly how much genetics and environment play a role in an individual's development.

Growth is both quantitative and qualitative: -

As a child develops physically, he also develops qualitatively in terms of his personality. That is to say, when a youngster grows older, his mental and emotional functions develop as well. As a result, these two qualities are inextricably linked.

Suggested Readings:

Brookshaw, S. (2009). The material culture of children and childhood: Understanding childhood objects in the museum context. Journal of Material Culture, 14(3), 365-383.

Ginsburg, I. (1982). Jean Piaget and Rudolf Steiner: Stages of child development and implications for pedagogy. Teachers College Record, 84(2), 327-337.

Bijou, S. W. (1976). Child development: The basic stage of early childhood.

Pem, D. (2015). Factors affecting early childhood growth and development: Golden 1000 days. Adv Practice Nurs, 1(101), 2573-0347.

CHAPTER THREE

Piaget's Concept of Cognitive Development

INTRODUCTION

COGNITIVE DEVELOPMENT

Cognitive development means how children think, explore and figure things out. It is the growth of information, skills, problem-solving abilities, and attitudes that enable children to think about and comprehend the world around them. Cognitive development includes brain development. Attention, short-term memory, long-term memory, logic & reasoning, auditory processing, visual processing, and processing speed are all cognitive capabilities. They are the abilities that the brain employs to think, learn, read, remember, focus, and solve issues.

Source: www.lumenlearning.com

Children gather, sort, and analyse data from their environment, which they then use to improve their perceptual and thinking skills. Early in life, the essential character of intelligence is established, and development entails the accumulation of increasingly more learning experiences.

VIEWS OF PIAGET, BRUNER AND VYGOTSKY ON COGNITIVE DEVELOPMENT

JEAN PIAGET

Source: www.thefamouspeople.com

During the twentieth century, Jean Piaget (1896-1980) was one of the most influential researchers in the field of developmental psychology. Piaget was educated in biology and philosophy and referred to himself as a "genetic epistemologist." He was particularly interested in biological influences on "how we learn." He claimed that our ability to undertake "abstract symbolic reasoning" is what sets us apart from other animals. Piaget's ideas are frequently contrasted with those of Lev Vygotsky (1896-1934), who saw social interaction as the major wellspring of cognition and behaviour. Piaget became interested in how children think while working at Binet's IQ test facility in Paris. He saw that young children's replies were qualitatively different from older children's, implying that the younger ones were not stupid than their older friends, but rather answered the questions differently because they thought differently. The importance of Piaget's ideas on child psychology today can be summarised by his views on education and teacher training. Although Jean Piaget's theory of cognitive development is well-known, most sociologists are unfamiliar with his name. Although Piaget was primarily interested in individual development, he felt that child-to-child interaction plays a role in cognitive development. Since the last formulations of Piaget's constructivism four decades ago, cognitive developmental psychology has undergone profound alterations. Theories of cognitive development have sparked long and bitter debates that have been heavy on rhetoric but light on facts. Piagetian views of cognitive development as arising from self-directed behaviour throughout infancy are the foundations of constructivist theory. Because Piaget's views on childhood were so well-known and accepted, at least one component of development seemed certain to many psychologists: human infants went through a long time in which they are unable to reason. They can learn to recognise items and grin at them, as well as crawl and control objects, but they lack conceptions and ideas. This time, which Piaget dubbed the sensorimotor stage of development, was thought to last until a child was one-and-a-half to two years old. Infants learn how to represent the world in a symbolic, conceptual man? Ner near the end of this stage, and thus progress from infancy to early childhood. According to Jean Piaget's theory of cognitive development, children's intellect evolves through time. A kid's cognitive growth entails more than just collecting information; the youngster must also create or develop a mental picture of the world. Piaget stressed universal cognitive change as a result.

JEROME SEYMOUR BRUNER

Source: www.washingtonpost.com

Bruner, Jerome Seymour, was an American psychologist who made significant contributions to human cognitive psychology and educational psychology's cognitive learning theory. Jerome Bruner, a psychologist by training, has always been and continues to be one of the most influential individuals in education. In the 1960s and 1970s, his educational philosophy had a direct impact on the educational programmes that were developed throughout those decades. Bruner believes that learners develop their own knowledge by employing a coding system to organise and categorise information. Bruner believed that discovering a coding system rather than being informed by a teacher is the most efficient approach to do so. Jerome Bruner was a key figure in the Cognitive Revolution, which brought behaviourism to an end in American psychology and put cognition at the forefront. Bruner argues for the primacy of 'meaning-making' in human action in his reassessment of the cognitive revolution, saying that toddlers learn to give meaning to what individuals do as they learn the language and social practices of their culture. The importance of attribution of mental states to others has been examined extensively in a new research area known as children's "theory of mind" over the last decade.

Unlike Bruner, who views psychology as a natural empirical science, researchers in this discipline consider the child as developing a causal theory to explain and predict human behaviour.

LEV SEMYONOVICH VYGOTSKY

Source: www.curriculumsolutions.com

Lev Semyonovich Vygotsky was a Soviet psychologist who specialised in child psychological development. Over the last several decades, Lev Vygotsky's (1934) work has served as the foundation for much research and theory in cognitive development, notably what has come to be known as sociocultural theory. Human development is viewed as a socially mediated process in which children acquire cultural values, beliefs, and problem-solving skills through collaborative conversations with more informed members of society, according to Vygotsky's sociocultural theory. Culture-specific tools, private speech, and the Zone of Proximal Development are all notions in Vygotsky's theory. Vygotsky's theories emphasise the importance of social contact in the formation of cognition (Vygotsky, 1978), since he strongly believed that community plays an important role in the process of "creating meaning."

Unlike Piaget, who believed that children's growth must come first, Vygotsky believed that "learning is an essential and universal part of the process of establishing culturally organised, specifically human psychological function." Vygotsky pioneered a sociocultural perspective on cognitive development. He formed his theories at roughly the same time that Jean Piaget was starting to develop his ideas (1920's and 30's), but he died at the age of 38, and so his theories remain incomplete – although some of his publications are currently being translated from Russian. Vygotsky emphasises the role of culture in cognitive development. Vygotsky believes that cognitive development differs by culture. Vygotsky lays a greater emphasis on the social aspects that influence cognitive development. For learning, Vygotsky emphasises the importance of cultural and social context. Children and their partners co-construct knowledge as a result of social interactions from guided learning within the zone of proximal development. Vygotsky emphasises the function of language in cognitive development more (and in a different way) than others. Cognitive development, according to Vygotsky, is the product of linguistic internalisation. Adults, according to Vygotsky, are a crucial source of cognitive development. Vygotsky stated that children are born with "elementary mental functions," which he defined as "fundamental skills for intellectual development." Vygotsky, like Piaget, believes that young children are naturally curious and actively involved in their own learning, as well as the discovery and development of new knowledge.

MORAL DEVELOPMENT

The psychology study of moral growth has grown significantly, both in terms of theoretical diversity and in terms of the number of theoretical viewpoints represented in the area. Children form configurations of thinking about welfare, justice, and rights linked to feelings like attachment, sympathy, and empathy, according to a structural developmental relational perspective. Children form systems of judgements in the domains of social convention, which include uniformities within social systems, and the personal domain, which involves understandings of permissible realms of choice, freedoms, and autonomy, in addition to moral judgments. Moral, conventional, and personal judgments are unique from one another in this social domain approach, and they form separate growth trajectories. Adulthood phases for moral growth are discussed after evaluating the qualities of the cognitive-developmental stage concept, which has previously been limited in its application to child and adolescent development. Other approaches to moral formation and accompanying basic psychological assumptions are compared to the structural relational domain approach. From birth through adulthood, moral development is concerned with the emergence, change, and comprehension of morality.

Morality develops during the course of a person's life and is influenced by their experiences and conduct when confronted with moral concerns at various stages of physical and cognitive development. In summary, morality is concerned with an individual's developing sense of what is good and wrong; as a result, young children's moral judgement and character differ from that of an adult. Morality is frequently used interchangeably with the terms "rightness" and "goodness." It refers to a code of conduct that guides one's activities, behaviours, and beliefs and is drawn from one's culture, religion, or personal philosophy.

LAWRENCE KOHLBERG

educationaltechnology.net

Lawrence Kohlberg was an American psychologist who is best known for his moral development phases theory. He devised a research programme to better understand moral development–which he referred to as justice development–over the course of a lifetime. Kohlberg investigated the stage of development and moral perspectives of children, adolescents, and adults in the United States and overseas using dilemma interviews and a detailed scoring manual. He talked about the relationship between judgement and action, the transnational universality of moral development, and gender-related morality in this context. His groundbreaking interdisciplinary work spanned subjects as diverse as developmental psychology, philosophy, and education, to name a few. His study was inspirational in many ways and will continue to be inspirational for years to come. Lawrence Kohlberg has been advancing his cognitive development hypothesis of moralization, which has become prominent in the study of moral development and its application to moral education, for nearly three decades. Kohlberg's moral development theory is concerned with how children learn morality and moral reasoning. According to Kohlberg's thesis, moral development develops in six stages.

The theory also suggests that moral logic is primarily focused on seeking and maintaining justice. Each stage offers a new perspective, but not everyone functions at the highest level all the time. There were three levels of moral reasoning that encompassed the six stages. The three levels were Pre-Conventional, Conventional and post conventional. The six stages are:

Stage 1: The first stage emphasizes children's self-interest in decision-making as they try to avoid punishment at all costs. Kohlberg considers children's moral thinking. They believe that regulations are expected to be observed at a young age, and that people in control will definitely punish them.

Stage 2: This stage examines how youngsters learn to embrace the viewpoints taught, while simultaneously acknowledging that there are several points of view on each topic. Each person is unique and, as a result, will have a distinct perspective based on their interests.

Stage 3: This stage acknowledges the desire to be accepted into societal groupings, as well as how the outcome affects each individual.

Stage 4: Laws and social order are supreme at this point. It is necessary to follow and obey the rules and regulations. Stage four depicts a person's moral growth as a member of a larger society. Everyone becomes more conscious of how their activities affect others and concentrates on their own position, following rules, and respecting authorities.

Stage 5: This stage acknowledges the introduction of abstract reasoning as people attempt to explain specific behaviors.

Stage 6: Moral reasoning is founded on personal values, according to the final step of Kohlberg's theory. When Kohlberg recognised that elected methods do not always provide fair outcomes, he created Stage 6. To acknowledge the application of justice in moral thinking, the sixth stage was formed. As a starting point for what is good and just, general, universal morality and ethics are applied. These are frequently abstract concepts that can only be sketched rather than defined. Universal principles are based on values like equality, fairness, dignity, and respect.

CONCLUSION

According to Kohlberg's findings, each stage of moral development occurs one at a time and in the same order. Moral growth is invariant; individuals progress through the phases one at a time and in a predetermined order, but some may never reach the ultimate level. He also came to the conclusion that the stages' order is universal across all cultures.

REFERENCES

Tudge, J., & Rogoff, B. (1999). Peer influences on cognitive development: Piagetian and Vygotskian perspectives. Lev Vygotsky: critical assessments, 3, 32-56.

Mandler, J. M. (1990). A new perspective on cognitive development in infancy. American Scientist, 78(3), 236-243.

Takaya, K. (2008). Jerome Bruner's theory of education: From early Bruner to later Bruner. Interchange, 39(1), 1-19.

Astington, J. W., & Olson, D. R. (1995). The cognitive revolution in children's understanding of mind. Human development, 38(4-5), 179-189.

Huitt, W., & Hummel, J. (2003). Piaget's theory of cognitive development. Educational psychology interactive, 3(2), 1-5.

McLeod, S. A. (2014). Lev vygotsky.

Piaget, J. (1965). The moral development. New York: Free Press, 1(1), 0.

Turiel, E. (2015). Moral development. Handbook of child psychology and developmental science, 1-39.

Kohlberg, L. (1986). Lawrence Kohlberg, consensus and controversy (No. 1). Routledge.

CHAPTER FOUR

Kohlberg's Theory of Moral Development

Introduction:

Every day in the course of life, we determine wrong-pure, right-wrong, etc. under the shelter of logic. Today, the one who is considered to be great, may be put in the seat of the gods, and after a few days, he may be dragged down again by the counter-argument.Although such differences in principles and ideologies depend on various factors, the idea of good and evil is formed in people from childhood.Infact, as a child gets older, logical thinking develops and the sense of morality is created by relying on logical thinking. Like adults, children take on the sounds, lights, subjects, events around them in their own way, think, analyze and, above all, make decisions about them.Morality is a fundamental element of a child's social development. Children develop their morals and values by taking on family members or friends as 'Models'. Moreover, family traditions, religious education, etc. also help them to develop morals.

Our sense of right-wrong, good-evil is called moral sense. This moral feeling tends to change as the person grows older. Researchers at the university of chicago in the 1950s detailed Kohlberg's moral development. The primary source of his research was the psychologist Piaget's experiments on moral development. I have discussed kohlberg's theory of moral development.

Concept of Moral Behaviour:

Moral behavior is to behave in a way that is socially fixed or socially desirable. The word 'Moral' is derived from the latin word 'Mores' which means to follow certain rules and regulations. Moral behaviour is governed by moral concepts.And this moral concept is a combination of the behaviour that a particular society expects from all its members. In the course of life, a person gains experience in the need for a sense of principle and puts principles in front of him according to certain rules.Again according to many since morality is an acquired trait of the individual it is possible to develop and control it by education.Most educators believe in the latter belief and consider ethics as one of the goals of education.

Moral Development in Learners:

Kohlberg made some changes to the Piaget method. He wants to know the children's decision by highlighting the situation of two conflicting moral judgments. Based on the results of his experiments, he rearranged the stages of Piaget moral development and presented his own information. According to him, moral development depends on the development of wisdom and with the development of wisdom, children learn to judge the good and evil of the things around them, on the basis of which moral development begins.

Kohlberg (1927-87) submitted his dissertation on the moral development of children for a doctorate from the university of chicago, USA. His research reveals the futility of traditional theories on moral development. After teaching for 6 years at the university of chicago, he was invited to teach at Harvard university, where he spent his life researching on moral development.Kohlberg says there are three key elements in the moral development of an individual's life.

1) **Cognitive Development:** Kohlberg speaks of Piaget's policy of cognitive development as a condition of moral development. He says Piaget's proposed developmental level helps the individual make socially based moral judgments. That is, a person's moral judgment depends on his cognitive development. But Kohlberg also states that cognitive development is not the only condition or cause of moral development.

2) **Moral Dilemma:** Another element that helps in moral development is moral dilemma. Conflicting the external environment with conflicting thoughts or beliefs of the individual leads to cognitive conflict. The process of cognitive conflict is conducive to the creative or moral development of the individual.

3) Moral Reasoning or role taking ability: Whether a person will be able to put an end to his or her conflict depends on an element. Kohlberg calls this element the ability to take on roles. The ability to take on this role depends especially on his/her previous social experience and through it he/she gains additional social experience.

Lawrence Kohlberg, a psychologist belonging to the University of Harvard is known for putting forward a theory of the development of moral judgement in the individual, right from the years of early childhood. He has based his theory of moral development on the findings of his studies conducted on hundreds of children from different cultures.

He differs from the popular view that children imbibe the sense and methods of moral judgement from their parents and elders by way of learning. According to him as soon as we talk with children about morality, we find that they have many ways of making judgements which are not internalized from the outside, and which do not come in any direct and obvious way from parents, teachers and even peels, (Kohlberg, 1968). Going further he clarified that internal or cognitive processes like thinking and reasoning also play a major role in one's moral development, i.e. the way children make moral judgement depends on their level of intellectual development as well as on their upbringing and learning experiences.

Meaning & Concept of Morality:

The word moral comes from the Latin word 'Mors', which means custom or practice or a way of accomplishing things. Therefore it has come to mean 'belonging to manners and conduct of men' or 'pertaining to right and wrong, good in conduct'. Morality is the conformity to the moral code of social group. It is the internalization of a set of values, virtues, and ideas sanctioned by the society which becomes an integral part of the individual self through the process of development. It is considered a sum total of an individual's way of behaving which is judged in terms of ethical rightness or wrongness.

The term 'Morality' stands for following the moral code of society or conformity in behaviour to the manners, values and customs of the social group. It also includes a sense of right or wrong. Morality consists of ideals or rules that govern human conduct Morality has a, social reference. Moral standards vary from group to group depending upon what has been accepted by the group as the socially approved behaviour. True morality comes from within the individual. It is internal in nature and not imposed by external authority.

Hence the ability to make moral judgement plays an important facet of the total development of the child. Moral judgement involves the cognitive capacity and insight to see the relationship between the abstract principle and concrete cases and judge the situations as right or wrong, keeping in view the knowledge of moral standards.

The theory which most directly inspired the research on moral judgement has been that of Swiss psychologist, Jean Piaget (1928, 1932) who endeavoured to interpret the child's concept of moral rules. He attempted to test children's moral judgement towards intentional and unintentional wrong-doing and described six types of moral thoughts which appeared in children of different age groups. More recently, studies on moral judgement have been conducted by Kohlberg (1968), in which he asked the children to judge the morality of conduct as described in the stories.

Different Educational Commissions and committees in our country have expressed their deep concern over the declining values in human activities and emphasized on providing value oriented education. The National Policy on Education-1986 has categorically stated "The growing concern over erosion of essential values has brought to focus the need for readjustment in the curriculum in order to make education a forceful tool for the cultivation of moral and social values". The Education Commission of 1964-66 has noted, "A serious defect in the school curriculum is the absence of provision for education in social, moral and spiritual values. In the life of the majority of Indians, religion is a great motivating force and is intimately bound up with the formation of character and inculcation of ethical values. A national system of education related to life needs and aspirations of the people cannot afford to ignore this purposeful force". Thus concerns are being expressed to inculcate right moral values in our present generation.

Meaning of Moral Development: Hemming in his book, "The Development of Children's Moral Values' writes, "Moral development is the process in which the child acquires the values esteemed by his community, acquires a sense of right and wrong in terms of these values, learns to regulate his personal desires and compulsions so that, when a situational conflict arises, he does, what he ought to do rather than what he wants to do. Moral development is the process by which a community seeks to transfer the egocentricity of the baby into the social behaviour of the mature adult."

Moral development includes moral behaviour and moral concepts:

Moral behaviour: Moral behaviour means behaviour in conformity with the moral code of the social group. The term 'Moral' comes from the Latin word 'mores' meaning manners, customs and folkways. Moral behaviour not only conforms to social standards but also it is carried out voluntarily. It is always accompanied by a feeling of responsibility for one's acts. It involves giving primary consideration to tile welfare of l he group and considering personal gain or desires as having secondary importance.

Moral concepts: Moral concepts arc the rules of‘ behaviour to which the members of a culture become accustomed and which determine the expected behaviour patterns of all group members.

Meaning of Moral Judgment: Moral judgments are evaluations or opinions formed as to whether some action or inaction, intention, motive, character trait, or a person as a whole is (more or less) good or bad as measured against some standard of Good. The moral judgments of actions (or inaction) are usually the primary focus of any discussion of Moral Judgments in particular and Ethical analysis in general. This is because the judgments of intentions, character traits, and persons are generally based on the judgment of actions that the intention, motive, character trait, or person might potentially do or not do.

What distinguishes moral judgments from non moral judgments is the context of the statement. Philosophy, and particularly Ethics, differs from the sciences in one very important way. All of the sciences, both ’hard‘ and "Soft’, deal with descriptions of Reality. They purport to describe in varying levels of detail, what is about Reality. Ethics, on the other hand, is that branch of Philosophy that describes what one ought. All of the various philosophers, in all of their various works on Ethics, are detailing what you "Should" do or how things "Should" be, not what is. In answer to the questions "What should I do?" or "What is the ‘right’ thing to do?", ethics answers "You should do what you ‘ought’ to!" So moral judgments are judgments about what one "ought" to do (or not do), or have done (or not done).

Types of Moral Judgement:

We can group moral judgments into two broad classes. There are "before-the-fact" moral judgments, and there are "after-the-fact" moral judgments. Before-the-fact judgments are those made before the action (or inaction) takes place. They are made based on the best information available at the time as to what the moral landscape holds and what its future shape will be. These are judgments about what you "ought to do (or not do) and whether what you are planning to do (or not do) is Good or Bad. After-the-fact moral judgments are made after the action (or inaction) has taken place, and are based on 20/20 hindsight view of the actual consequences. These are judgments about what you "ought to have done (or not done)", and whether your actual actions were Good or Bad.

A second major distinction of moral judgments is that they can only be made of an agent with the freedom or will to choose. Moral judgments are judgments of certain choices, or potential choices, where the one who chooses is aware that there is a choice, and has the capability to choose. A person who cannot do other than what was done, is not subject to moral judgment. But if a person has the freedom to choose alternatives, then that person's intentional, or unintentional actions or inaction can be subject to moral judgments. This argument is the ethical basis of the "Insanity" defence. The insanity defence argues that the accused cannot be considered guilty because the accused was unable to make a choice of an alternate behaviour. The behaviour exhibited was "unavoidable". This line of reasoning is never too successful when it is applied to the average human, with an average degree of intelligence. But it is the reason we do not make moral judgments about what a falling tree does on its way down. If the tree happens to kill someone, we don't judge that the tree "ought not to have done that" because the tree had no other alternative.

The third important distinction is knowledge. In order to be able to make a choice, we have to be aware that there are alternatives. If our knowledge about our current situation is thin, or our knowledge about how reality behaves is thin, then we might come to the conclusion that there are no better alternatives. We might make a choice that we believe is the correct one, but because our knowledge is thin, we overlook a better one. In such a case, we could make an after-the-fact judgment about what we ought to have done, if we had had better information, but any before-the-fact moral judgment we might make about what we did, has to be based on the knowledge available to us at that time.

Theories of Moral Development: Moral development is one of the most significant aspects of the personality development. It is a major task of society and education. Moral development proceeds along with social development. A person whose social development has been disturbed due to some, or the other reason, a person who is socially maladjusted develops immoral behaviour.

Immoral behaviour is that behaviour which fails to conform to social expectations. Such behaviour arises not due to ignorance of social aspect ions, but due to intentional disapproval of social standards or lack of feelings of obligation to conform. Similarly a person who has been deprived of opportunity to learn social standards or lack of feelings of obligation to conform. Similarly a person who has been deprived of the opportunity to learn social behaviour develops unmoral or non-moral behaviour. Unmoral or non moral behaviour arises due to ignorance of what the social group expects rather than intentional violation of the group's standards.

Stages of Moral Development:

For studying the process of moral development in human beings, Kohlberg first defined moral development as the development of an individual's sense of justice. For estimating one's sense of justice he concentrated on one's views on morality with the help of a test of moral judgement consisting of a set of moral dilemmas. For instance, should a man who cannot afford the medicine his dying wife needs, steal it? Should a doctor mercy-kill a fatally ill person suffering terrible pain? Is it better to save the life of one important person or a lot of unimportant persons? With the help of the responses he got from his subjects he came to the conclusion that like the Piagetial stages of cognitive development, there also exist universal stages in the development of moral values, and the movement from one stage to another depends on cognitive abilities rather than the simple acquisition of moral values of one's parents, elders and peers. He then identified three levels of moral development, each containing two stages as shown in the following table:

Table: Kohlberg's Six Stages of Moral Development

Table: Kohlberg's Six Stages of Moral Development

Level I	Pre-moral (Age 4 to 10 years)
Stage 1 :	The stage of obedience for avoiding punishment
Stage 2 :	The stage of conforming to obtain rewards and favours in return
Level II	Conventional morality (Age 10 to 13 years)
Stage 3 :	The stage of maintaining mutual relations and approval of others
Stage 4 :	The stage of obedience for avoiding censure by higher authority or social systems
Level III	Self accepted moral principles (Age 13 or not until middle or later adulthood or never)
Stage 5:	Stage of conforming to the democratically accepted law and mores of community welfare
Stage 6:	Stage of conforming to the universal ethical principles and the call of one's conscience

id.pinterest.com

Let us now briefly discuss these levels and stages of morality.

Pre-moral level (4 to 10 years). The child begins to make judgements about what is right or wrong, good or bad. However, the standards by which he measures the morality are those of others. He is persuaded to take such judgement either to avoid punishment or to earn rewards. Development of morality at this level usually follows the following two stages:

Stage 1: In the beginning, the child's morality is controlled by the fear of punishment. He tries to obey his parents and elders purely to avoid reproof and punishment.

Stage 2; In the second stage of the pre-moral level, children's moral judgement is based on self-interest and considerations of what others can do for them in return. Here they value a thing because it has some practical utility for them. They obey the orders of their parents and elders and abide by some rules and regulations, because it serves their interests.

Conventional morality level (10 to 13 years). At this stage also, children's moral Judgement is controlled by the likes and dislikes of others-the conventions, rules and regulations and the law and order system maintained within society. Stealing or mercy-killing would thus be judged wrong because it is considered wrong by society at large and by the legal system. In this way, the conventional level of morality may be regarded as the level where the child identifies with authority. It is characterized by the following two stages:

Stage 3: In the early years of the second level of moral development, the child's moral judgement is based on the desire to obtain approval of others and avoid being disliked by being declared a good boy or a good girl. For this purpose he begins to judge the intentions and likes or dislikes of others and acts accordingly.

Stage 4: In the later years of the conventional morality level, children's moral judgements are governed by conventions as well as the laws and mores of the social system. The standards of others are now so established that it becomes a convention to follow them. The children now follow the rules and regulations of society and take decisions about things being right or wrong with a view to avoiding censure by the elders, authorities or the social system.

Self-accepted moral principles level (Age 13 or during late adulthood). This marks the highest level of attainment of true morality as the controlling force for making moral judgements now rests with the individual himself. He does not value a thing or conform to an idea merely because of consideration of the views of others, conventions or the law and order system of society but because it fits into the framework of his self-accepted moral principles. This level is also characterized by two separate stages:

Stage 5: At this stage the individual's moral judgements are internalized in such a form that he responds positively to authority only if he agrees with the principles upon which the demands of authority are based. The individual at this stage begins to think in rational terms, valuing the rights of human beings and the welfare of society. For example, at this stage in deference to the rights of the human being, the decision about mercy-killing may be left to the individual who is suffering, and if so needed, the concerned laws may be amended for the welfare of society at large.

Stage 6: At this stage, the controlling forces for making moral judgements are highly internalized. The decisions of the individual are now based upon his conscience and the belief in universal principles of respect, justice and equality. He does what he, as an individual thinks right regardless of legal restrictions or the opinion of others. Thus, at this stage people act according to the inner voice of their conscience and lead a life that they can without self-condemnation or feeling of guilt or shame.

Kohlberg chose a few features of human nature as the basis of his doctrine. The features are as follows:

A) He originally tried to explain the process of moral development, so he did not specifically mention the development of childhood, but he did admit that in childhood, a person has some cognitive development.As a result of this development he /she can distinguish between the material environment and the human environment or the social environment. The main feature of the human environment is where interactions take place, this interaction is the basis of moral development.

B) Kohlberg says there is no provocative center of moral conduct. By Conscience he means justice or fairness. Therefore, for him, the sense of conscience is rational, that is, according to him, moral development is a kind of cognitive development.

C) Kohlberg says of human nature that they can distinguish between their own manifest behaviour, intention of behaviour, and the intrinsic effect of this behaviour.These three powers of man, according to Kohlberg, contribute to his moral development.

Kohlberg's model of Moral Development:

In one of his essays, published in 1984, Kohlberg divided people into two groups in terms of moral development. These are discussed below:

1) A type: Kohlberg says that the influence of authority and rules on moral development can be noticed in some individuals. These individuals do not perform moral behaviour very spontaneously. These people are classified as A.

2) B type: There are some people who manage their own moral behaviour in terms of an improved way of life. Among them is the spontaneity of moral conduct. They are classified as B

Kohlberg says that in moral development there is a tendency for class A people to be promoted to class B, but there is no tendency for class B people to be class A. In most cases, however, individuals try to maintain their own class characteristics during moral development.

The application of kohlberg's theory in the field of education is extremely important for the benefit of both the individual and society. Kohlberg himself has taken moral development seriously in education and has discussed strategies for moral development.According to kohlberg, the most important aspect of moral development is moral conflict. So the teacher will raise the issue of moral conflict in the classroom as much as possible.

The teacher can take the following steps in this regard

1) The difference in the intellectual meaning of the students in the classroom is conducive to the onset of moral conflict. That is why teachers and students should be informed about their intellectual value.

2) The classroom environment will be one where students can openly discuss ethical conflicts. The teacher can exercise his authority as required in making any decision regarding the lower moral conflict. However, the teacher will ensure that the older students in the upper class end the moral conflict through mutual discussion and exchange of trust.

3) Confidence in students and their opinions need to be taken seriously. Ethical education is more effective by teachers who are dear to the students and who have a sweet relationship with the students.

4) It is not easy to build trust between students and sweet student-teacher relationship. Enough time is needed to be aware of the individual teacher's assessment and how he or she will treat the student. It takes time for the teacher to see how sensitive the situation is and to see if the student's thoughts are normal.The teacher will be aware of this and after gaining the necessary experience, he will take appropriate measures to implement the

ethics.

5) Teachers will be sensitive about students' attitudes. If a student is emotionally traumatized during a discussion on moral conflict, the teacher will discuss and advise him / her separately. The teacher will encourage the student to express himself freely.

Kohlberg chose a few features of human nature as the basis of his doctrine. The features are as follows:

A) He originally tried to explain the process of moral development, so he did not specifically mention the development of childhood, but he did admit that in childhood, a person has some cognitive development.As a result of this development he /she can distinguish between the material environment and the human environment or the social environment. The main feature of the human environment is where interactions take place, this interaction is the basis of moral development.

B) Kohlberg says there is no provocative center of moral conduct. By Conscience he means justice or fairness. Therefore, for him, the sense of conscience is rational, that is, according to him, moral development is a kind of cognitive development.

C) Kohlberg says of human nature that they can distinguish between their own manifest behaviour, intention of behaviour, and the intrinsic effect of this behaviour.These three powers of man, according to Kohlberg, contribute to his moral development.

Kohlberg's model of Moral Development:

In one of his essays, published in 1984, Kohlberg divided people into two groups in terms of moral development. These are discussed below:

1) A type: Kohlberg says that the influence of authority and rules on moral development can be noticed in some individuals. These individuals do not perform moral behaviour very spontaneously. These people are classified as A.

2) B type: There are some people who manage their own moral behaviour in terms of an improved way of life. Among them is the spontaneity of moral conduct. They are classified as B

Kohlberg says that in moral development there is a tendency for class A people to be promoted to class B, but there is no tendency for class B people to be class A. In most cases, however, individuals try to maintain their own class characteristics during moral development.

Significance of Moral Development in Education:

The application of kohlberg's theory in the field of education is extremely important for the benefit of both the individual and society. Kohlberg himself has taken moral development seriously in education and has discussed strategies for moral development.According to kohlberg, the most important aspect of moral development is moral conflict. So the teacher will raise the issue of moral conflict in the classroom as much as possible.

The teacher can take the following steps in this regard

1) The difference in the intellectual meaning of the students in the classroom is conducive to the onset of moral conflict. That is why teachers and students should be informed about their intellectual value.

2) The classroom environment will be one where students can openly discuss ethical conflicts. The teacher can exercise his authority as required in making any decision regarding the lower moral conflict. However, the teacher will ensure that the older students in the upper class end the moral conflict through mutual discussion and exchange of trust.

3) Confidence in students and their opinions need to be taken seriously. Ethical education is more effective by teachers who are dear to the students and who have a sweet relationship with the students.

4) It is not easy to build trust between students and sweet student-teacher relationship. Enough time is needed to be aware of the individual teacher's assessment and how he or she will treat the student. It takes time for the teacher to see how sensitive the situation is and to see if the student's thoughts are normal.The teacher will be aware of this and after gaining the necessary experience, he will take appropriate measures to implement the ethics.

5) Teachers will be sensitive about students' attitudes. If a student is emotionally traumatized during a discussion on moral conflict, the teacher will discuss and advise him / her separately. The teacher will encourage the student to express himself freely.

Conclusion:

From the above discussion of the stages of moral development, it is clear that although children begin to think about morality in terms of justice or right and wrong at a very early age, yet they have to wait until adolescence or adulthood for the dawning of the stage of true morality. Also, it is not essential that all people pass through the third level of moral development. Most adults are not able to cross the second level and few can reach stage 5, and among these there are very few who, being intellectually quite sound, can think rationally and base their moral judgement purely on the dictates of their conscience at the risk of life and property.

CHAPTER FIVE

Erik Erikson's Stages of Psychosocial Development

Introduction'

Erik Erikson was an ego psychologist who developed one of the most popular and influential theories of development. While his theory was impacted by psychoanalyst Sigmund Freud's work, Erikson's theory centered on psychosocial development rather than psychosexual development.

Erikson's Stages of Psychosocial Development is a theory introduced in the 1950s by the psychologist and psychoanalyst Erik Erikson. It built upon Freud's theory of psychosexual development by drawing parallels in childhood stages while expanding it to include the influence of social dynamics as well as the extension of psychosocial development into adulthood.[1] It posits eight sequential stages of individual human development influenced by biological, psychological, and social factors throughout the lifespan. This bio-psychosocial approach has influenced several fields of study, including gerontology, personality development, identity formation, life cycle development, and more

The stages that make up his theory are as follows:

Stage 1: Trust vs. Mistrust

Stage 2: Autonomy vs. Shame and Doubt

Stage 3: Initiative vs. Guilt

Stage 4: Industry vs. Inferiority

Stage 5: Identity vs. Confusion

Stage 6: Intimacy vs. Isolation

Stage 7: Generativity vs. Stagnation

Stage 8: Integrity vs. Despair

Let's take a closer look at the background and different stages that make up Erikson's psychosocial theory.

Stage 1. Trust vs. Mistrust

Trust vs. mistrust is the first stage in Erik Erikson's theory of psychosocial development. This stage begins at birth continues to approximately 18 months of age. During this stage, the infant is uncertain about the world in which they live, and looks towards their primary caregiver for stability and consistency of care.

If the care the infant receives is consistent, predictable and reliable, they will develop a sense of trust which will carry with them to other relationships, and they will be able to feel secure even when threatened.

If these needs are not consistently met, mistrust, suspicion, and anxiety may develop.

If the care has been inconsistent, unpredictable and unreliable, then the infant may develop a sense of mistrust, suspicion, and anxiety. In this situation the infant will not have confidence in the world around them or in their abilities to influence events.

Stage 2. Autonomy vs. Shame and Doubt

Autonomy versus shame and doubt is the second stage of Erik Erikson's stages of psychosocial development. This stage occurs between the ages of 18 months to approximately 3 years. According to Erikson, children at this stage are focused on developing a sense of personal control over physical skills and a sense of independence.

Success in this stage will lead to the virtue of will. If children in this stage are encouraged and supported in their increased independence, they become more confident and secure in their own ability to survive in the world.

If children are criticized, overly controlled, or not given the opportunity to assert themselves, they begin to feel inadequate in their ability to survive, and may then become overly dependent upon others, lack self-esteem, and feel a sense of shame or doubt in their abilities.

Erikson states it is critical that parents allow their children to explore the limits of their abilities within an encouraging environment which is tolerant of failure.

For example, rather than put on a child's clothes a supportive parent should have the patience to allow the child to try until they succeed or ask for assistance.

So, the parents need to encourage the child to become more independent while at the same time protecting the child so that constant failure is avoided.

A delicate balance is required from the parent.

Stage 3. Initiative vs. Guilt

Initiative versus guilt is the third stage of Erik Erikson's theory of psychosocial development. During the initiative versus guilt stage, children assert themselves more frequently through directing play and other social interaction.

These are particularly lively, rapid-developing years in a child's life. According to Bee (1992), it is a "time of vigor of action and of behaviors that the parents may see as aggressive."

During this period the primary feature involves the child regularly interacting with other children at school. Central to this stage is play, as it provides children with the opportunity to explore their interpersonal skills through initiating activities.

Children begin to plan activities, make up games, and initiate activities with others. If given this opportunity, children develop a sense of initiative and feel secure in their ability to lead others and make decisions.

Stage 4:Industry vs. Inferiority

The fourth psychosocial stage takes place during the early school years from approximately ages 5 to 11. Through social interactions, children begin to develop a sense of pride in their accomplishments and abilities.

Children need to cope with new social and academic demands. Success leads to a sense of competence, while failure results in feelings of inferiority.

Children who are encouraged and commended by parents and teachers develop a feeling of competence and belief in their skills. Those who receive little or no encouragement from parents, teachers, or peers will doubt their abilities to be successful.

Successfully finding a balance at this stage of psychosocial development leads to the strength known as competence, in which children develop a belief in their abilities to handle the tasks set before them.

Stage 5: Identity vs. Confusion

The fifth psychosocial stage takes place during the often turbulent teenage years. This stage plays an essential role in developing a sense of personal identity which will continue to influence behavior and development for the rest of a person's life. Teens need to develop a sense of self and personal identity. Success leads to an ability to stay true to yourself, while failure leads to role confusion and a weak sense of self.

During adolescence, children explore their independence and develop a sense of self.2 Those who receive proper encouragement and reinforcement through personal exploration will emerge from this stage with a strong sense of self and feelings of independence and control. Those who remain unsure of their beliefs and desires will feel insecure and confused about themselves and the future.

What Is Identity?

When psychologists talk about identity, they are referring to all of the beliefs, ideals, and values that help shape and guide a person's behavior. Completing this stage successfully leads to fidelity, which Erikson described as an ability to live by society's standards and expectations.

While Erikson believed that each stage of psychosocial development was important, he placed a particular emphasis on the development of ego identity. Ego identity is the conscious sense of self that we develop through social interaction and becomes a central focus during the identity versus confusion stage of psychosocial development.

According to Erikson, our ego identity constantly changes due to new experiences and information we acquire in our daily interactions with others. As we have new experiences, we also take on challenges that can help or hinder the development of identity.

Why Identity Is Important

Our personal identity gives each of us an integrated and cohesive sense of self that endures through our lives. Our sense of personal identity is shaped by our experiences and interactions with others, and it is this identity that helps guide our actions, beliefs, and behaviors as we age.

Stage 6: Intimacy vs. Isolation

Young adults need to form intimate, loving relationships with other people. Success leads to strong relationships, while failure results in loneliness and isolation. This stage covers the period of early adulthood when people are exploring personal relationships.2

Erikson believed it was vital that people develop close, committed relationships with other people. Those who are successful at this step will form relationships that are enduring and secure.

Building On Earlier Stages

Remember that each step builds on skills learned in previous steps. Erikson believed that a strong sense of personal identity was important for developing intimate relationships. Studies have demonstrated that those with a poor sense of self tend to have less committed relationships and are more likely to struggler with emotional isolation, loneliness, and depression.

Successful resolution of this stage results in the virtue known as love. It is marked by the ability to form lasting, meaningful relationships with other people.

Stage 7: Generativity vs. Stagnation

Adults need to create or nurture things that will outlast them, often by having children or creating a positive change that benefits other people. Success leads to feelings of usefulness and accomplishment, while failure results in shallow involvement in the world.

During adulthood, we continue to build our lives, focusing on our career and family. Those who are successful during this phase will feel that they are contributing to the world by being active in their home and community.2 Those who fail to attain this skill will feel unproductive and uninvolved in the world.

Care is the virtue achieved when this stage is handled successfully. Being proud of your accomplishments, watching your children grow into adults, and developing a sense of unity with your life partner are important accomplishments of this stage.

Stage 8: Integrity vs. Despair

The final psychosocial stage occurs during old age and is focused on reflecting back on life.2 At this point in development, people look back on the events of their lives and determine if they are happy with the life that they lived or if they regret the things they did or didn't do.

Erikson's theory differed from many others because it addressed development throughout the entire lifespan, including old age. Older adults need to look back on life and feel a sense of fulfillment. Success at this stage leads to feelings of wisdom, while failure results in regret, bitterness, and despair.

At this stage, people reflect back on the events of their lives and take stock. Those who look back on a life they feel was well-lived will feel satisfied and ready to face the end of their lives with a sense of peace. Those who look back and only feel regret will instead feel fearful that their lives will end without accomplishing the things they feel they should have.

Those who are unsuccessful during this stage will feel that their life has been wasted and may experience many regrets. The person will be left with feelings of bitterness and despair.

As we grow older (65+ yrs) and become seniour citizens, we tend to slow down our productivity and explore life as a retired person.

Erik Erikson believed if we see our lives as unproductive, feel guilt about our past, or feel that we did not accomplish our life goals, we become dissatisfied with life and develop despair, often leading to depression and hopelessness.

Success in this stage will lead to the virtue of wisdom. Wisdom enables a person to look back on their life with a sense of closure and completeness, and also accept death without fear.

Hence,Wise people are not characterized by a continuous state of ego integrity, but they experience both ego integrity and despair. Thus, late life is characterized by both integrity and despair as alternating states that need to be balanced.

By extending the notion of personality development across the lifespan, Erikson outlines a more realistic perspective of personality development (McAdams, 2001).

Based on Erikson's ideas, psychology has reconceptualized the way the later periods of life are viewed. Middle and late adulthood are no longer viewed as irrelevant, because of Erikson, they are now considered active and significant times of personal growth.

One of the strengths of psychosocial theory is that it provides a broad framework from which to view development throughout the entire lifespan. It also allows us to emphasize the social nature of human beings and the important influence that social relationships have on development.

Researchers have found evidence supporting Erikson's ideas about identity and have further identified different sub-stages of identity formation.Some research also suggests that people who form strong personal identities during adolescence are better capable of forming intimate relationships during early adulthood. Other research suggests, however, that identity formation and development continues well into adulthood.

CHAPTER SIX

Gagne's Hierarchy of Learning

Introduction

In 1956, the American educational psychologist Robert M. Gagné proposed a system of classifying different types of learning in terms of the degree of complexity of the mental processes involved. He identified eight basic types, and arranged these in the hierarchy shown in Figure 1. According to Gagné, the higher orders of learning in this hierarchy build upon the lower levels, requiring progressively greater amounts of previous learning for their success. The lowest four orders tend to focus on the more behavioral aspects of learning, while the highest four focus on the more cognitive aspects.

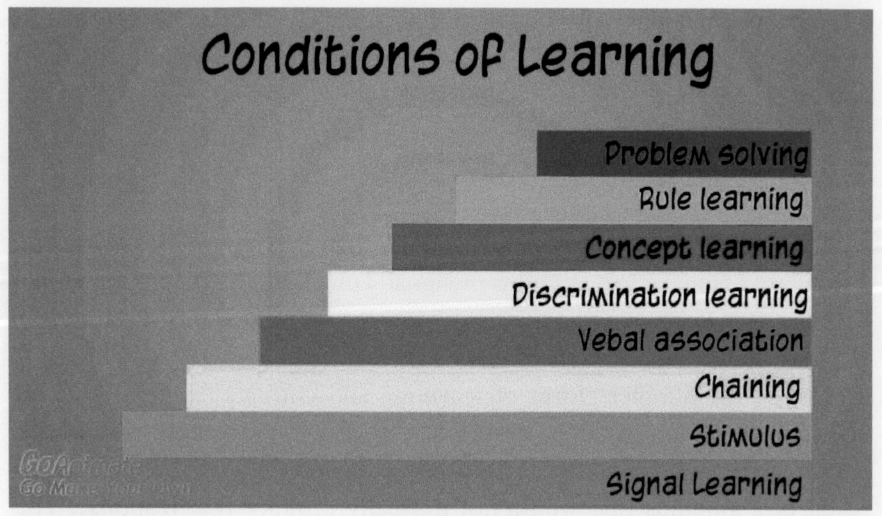

edtechbooks.org

The classification of learning according to Robert Gagné includes five categories of learned capabilities: intellectual skills, cognitive strategies, verbal information, attitudes, and motor skills. Out of these five categories of learning outcomes, intellectual skills are the only category that is divided into sub-categories. Gagné distinguished eight different classes of intellectual skills in which human beings learn in terms of the degree of complexity of the mental processes involved. He identified eight basic types, and arranged these in the hierarchy. According to Gagne, the higher orders of learning in this hierarchy build upon the lower levels, requiring progressively greater amounts of previous learning for their success. The lowest four orders tend to focus on the more behavioural aspects of learning, while the highest four focus on the more cognitive aspects.

Learning has been defined as a relatively permanent change in a behavioral tendency, the result of reinforced practice. Learning, an inferred state of organism, should be distinguished from performance, an observed state of the organism, should be distinguished from performance, an observed state of the organism. Learning events consist of stimuli, learner and responses.

He identified eight basic types, and arranged these in the hierarchy. According to Gagné, the higher orders of learning in this hierarchy build upon the lower levels, requiring progressively greater amounts of previous learning for their success. The lowest four orders tend to focus on the more behavioral aspects of learning, while the highest four focus on the more cognitive aspects.

- **Signal learning**

The first one is straightforward conditioning in which we learn to make a standard response to a stimulus or signal. For example, when a car sounds the horn as we are crossing the road, our eyes swivel towards the source of the noise and we quicken our steps.

This is the simplest form of learning, and consists essentially of the classical conditioning first described by the behavioural psychologist Pavlov. In this, the subject is ‘conditioned’ to emit a desired response as a result of a stimulus that would not normally produce that response. This is done by first exposing the subject to the chosen stimulus (known as the conditioned stimulus) along with another stimulus (known as the unconditioned stimulus) which produces the desired response naturally;

after a certain number of repetitions of the double stimulus, it is found that the subject emits the desired response when exposed to the conditioned stimulus on its own. The applications of classical conditioning in facilitating human learning are, however, very limited.

- **Stimulus-response learning**

This somewhat more sophisticated form of learning, which is also known as operant conditioning, was originally developed by Skinner.In this kind of learning, exemplified by animal training, the animal makes precise responses to specific stimuli. At first this training usually requires the use of a leash and a choke chain. As the dog learns particular responses for particular jerks of the leash and chain, his master rewards him with pats and praise. Later the master does not have to use the leash and chain; the animal sits, stays, or lies down upon hearing the simple verbal command. Whereas the responses in signal learning are diffuse and emotional, the responses in stimulus-response learning (often called operant conditioning) are fairly precise. Stimulus-response (SàR) learning may be used in acquiring verbal skills as well as physical movements. For example , the child may learn to say "Mama" on request, or an adult may learn the appropriate response to the stimulus of a word in a foreign language.

- **Chaining**

It is the process of connecting together a number of learnt responses into a sequence. Gagne describes two kinds of chaining. The first is motor chaining – learning a skill such as riding a bike – and the second is verbal chaining – rote learning a regulation or a saying or a time table. Verbal chaining is one of the key processes in the development of language skills.

These kinds of learning are basic ones and therefore appear at the bottom of the hierarchy. But they are the type that we engage in all the time, and so can occur alongside other kinds of learning further up the hierarchy. Gagne argues that the kinds of learning lower down in the hierarchy form prerequisites for the kinds of learning further up the hierarchy.

- **Verbal association**

This is a form of chaining in which the links between the items being connected are verbal in nature. Verbal association is one of the key processes in the development of language skills.This learning is a type of chaining, but the links are verbal units. The simplest verbal association is the activity of naming an object, which involves a chain of two links: An observing response enables the child to identify properly the object he sees; and an internal stimulus enables the child to say the proper name. When the child can name an object "ball" and also say " the red ball" he has learned a vernal association of three links. Gagne calls another common verbal association translation responses; in these the learner frequently acquires verbal associations by verbal mediation- an internal link which helps him associate.

- **Discrimination learning**

This involves developing the ability to make appropriate (different) responses to a series of similar stimuli that differ in a systematic way. The process is made more complex (and hence more difficult) by the phenomenon of interference, whereby one piece of learning inhibits another. Interference is thought to be one of the main causes of forgetting.In this type of learning the student must learn different responses for stimuli which might be confused. The student learns to distinguish between motor and verbal chains he has already acquired. Teachers, Gagne suggests, engage in discrimination learning when the devise means for calling each student by his correct name.

- **Concept learning**

This involves developing the ability to make a consistent response to different stimuli that form a common class or category of some sort. It forms the basis of the ability to generalise, classify etc.In learning a concept we respond to stimuli in terms of abstract characteristics like color, shape, position and number as opposed to concrete physical properties like specific wavelengths or particular intensities. In concept learning the student's behavior is not under the control of particular physical stimuli but of the abstract properties of each stimulus. Concepts have concrete references even though they are learned with the use of language.

- **Rule learning**

Rule learning describes the ability to respond to a class of stimuli with a class of performances. This is a very-high-level cognitive process that involves being able to learn relationships between concepts and apply these relationships in different situations, including situations not previously encountered. It forms the basis of the learning of general rules, procedures, etc. An example of rule learning would be when we can demonstrate the ability to write nouns in the plural. For Gagne, therefore, a rule allows us to behave in a consistent or regular way in the face of a variety of events or phenomena.

- **Problem-solving**

This is the highest level of cognitive process according to Gagné. It involves developing the ability to invent a complex rule, algorithm or procedure for the purpose of solving one particular problem, and then using the method to solve other problems of a similar nature.

In the set of events called problem solving, individuals use rule to achieve some goal. When the goal is reached, however the student has learned something more and is then capable of new performances using his new knowledge. What is learned, is a higher order rule, the combined product of two or more lower order rules. Thus the problem solving requires those internal events usually called thinking.. Without knowledge of the prerequisite rules, the problem can not be solved.

The most complete description of Gagne's classes of behavior appears his 'The conditions of learning'. Here he distinguishes eight types of learning, beginning with the simple forms and ending with the complex. Although he refers to these classes as learning types, he is primarily interested in the observable behavior and performance which ware the products of each such class.

Educational Implications:

1. **Gain Attention:** The first event or step of instruction is to gain attention to get the reception of stimuli.

2 **Informing the learners the objective:** it is important to inform the learner of the purpose and expected outcome of the learning to provide the motivation to learners.

3. **Stimulating recall of prior learning:** the learners are asked to recall the existing relevant knowledge.

4. **Presenting the stimulus:** relevant stimulus to the subject matter should be presented.

5. **Providing learning guidance:** it request instructor to make the stimulus as meaningful as possible.

6. **Eliciting performance:** the learners are asked to demonstrate the newly learnt behaviour.

7. **Providing feedback:** giving informative feedback to learners performance is important.

8. **Assessing performance:** it consists of assessments to verify the learning has occurred.

9. **Enhancing retention and transfer:** it refers to retaining the land capability over a long period of time and transferring it to new situations outside the learning environment.

While Gagne's theoretical framework covers all aspects of learning, the focus of the theory is on intellectual skills. The theory has been applied to the design of instruction in all domains (Gagner & Driscoll, 1988). In its original formulation (Gagne, 1 962), special attention was given to military training settings. Gagne (1987) addresses the role of instructional technology in learning.

References:

- Gagne, R. (1985). The Conditions of Learning (4th ed.). New York: Holt, Rinehart & Winston .
- Gagne, R. (1987). Instructional Technology Foundations. Hillsdale, NJ: Lawrence Erlbaum Assoc.
- Gagne, R. & Driscoll, M. (1988). Essentials of Learning for Instruction (2nd Ed.). Englewood Cliffs, NJ: Prentice-Hall.
- Gagne, R., Briggs, L. & Wager, W. (1992). Principles of Instructional Design (4th Ed.). Fort Worth, TX: HBJ College Publishers.
- http://www.vkmaheshwari.com/WP/?p=854
- https://enfercognitionis.blogspot.com/2019/03/gagnes-eight-level-of-learning.html
- https://icebreakerideas.com/learning-theories/

CHAPTER SEVEN

Drive-Reduction Theory and Human Behavior

Introduction

The drive reduction theory of motivation became popular during the 1940s and 1950s as a way to explain behavior, learning, and motivation. The theory was created by behaviorist Clark Hull and further developed by his collaborator Kenneth Spence. According to the theory, the reduction of drives is the primary force behind motivation.

While the drive-reduction theory of motivation was once a dominant force in psychology, it is largely ignored today. Despite this, it's worthwhile for students to learn more about Hull's ideas in order to understand the effect his work had on psychology and to see how other theorists responded by proposing their own theories.

Discussion

Hull was one of the first theorists to attempt to create a grand theory designed to explain all behavior. He started developing his theory shortly after he began working at Yale University, drawing on ideas from a number of other thinkers including Charles Darwin, Ivan Pavlov, John. B. Watson, and Edward L. Thorndike.

Hull based his theory on the concept of homeostasis, the idea that the body actively works to maintain a certain state of balance or equilibrium. For example, your body regulates its temperature in order to ensure that you don't become too hot or too cold. Hull believed that behavior was one of the ways that an organism maintains this balance.

Based on this idea, Hull suggested that all motivation arises as a result of these biological needs. In his theory, Hull used the term drive to refer to the state of tension or arousal caused by biological or physiological needs. Thirst, hunger, and the need for warmth are all examples of drives. A drive creates an unpleasant state, a tension that needs to be reduced.

In order to reduce this state of tension, humans and animals seek out ways to fulfill these biological needs. We get a drink when we are thirsty. We eat when we are hungry. We turn up the thermostat when we are cold. He suggested that humans and animals will then repeat any behavior that reduces these drives.

Conditioning and Reinforcement

Hull is considered a neo-behaviorist thinker, but like the other major behaviorists, he believed that human behavior could be explained by conditioning and reinforcement. The reduction of the drive acts as a reinforcement for that behavior.

This reinforcement increases the likelihood that the same behavior will occur again in the future when the same need arises. In order to survive in its environment, an organism must behave in ways that meet these survival needs.

"When survival is in jeopardy, the organism is in a state of need (when the biological requirements for survival are not being met) so the organism behaves in a fashion to reduce that need," Hull explained.

In a stimulus-response (S-R) relationship, when the stimulus and response are followed by a reduction in the need, it increases the likelihood that the same stimulus will elicit the same response again in the future.

Mathematical Behavior

Hull's goal was to develop a theory of learning that could be expressed mathematically, to create a "formula" to explain and understand human behavior.

Mathematical Deductive Theory of Behavior

- sEr = V x D x K x J x sHr - sIr - Ir - sOr - sLr
- sEr: Excitatory potential, or the likelihood that an organism will produce a response (r) to a stimulus (s)
- V: Stimulus intensity dynamism, meaning some stimuli will have greater influences than others
- D: Drive strength, determined by the amount of biological deprivation
- K: Incentive motivation, or the size or magnitude of the goal
- J: The delay before the organism is allowed to seek reinforcement
- sHr: Habit strength, established by the amount of previous conditioning
- slr: Conditioned inhibition, caused by previous lack of reinforcement
- lr: Reactive inhibition, or fatigue

- sOr: Random error
- sLr: Reaction threshold, or the smallest amount of reinforcement that will produce learning

Hull's approach was viewed by many as overly complex, yet at the same time, critics suggested that the drive-reduction theory failed to fully explain human motivation. His work did, however, have an influence on psychology and future theories of motivation.

Contemporary Criticism

While Hull's theory was popular during the middle part of the 20th century, it began to fall out of favor for a number of reasons. Because of his emphasis on quantifying his variables in such a narrowly defined way, his theory lacks generalizability. However, his emphasis on rigorous experimental techniques and scientific methods did have an important influence in the field of psychology.

One of the biggest problems with Hull's drive reduction theory is that it does not account for how secondary reinforcers reduce drives.

Unlike primary drives such as hunger and thirst, secondary reinforcers do nothing to directly reduce physiological and biological needs. Take money, for example. While money does allow you to purchase primary reinforcers, it does nothing in and of itself to reduce drives. Despite this, money still acts as a powerful source of reinforcement.

Another major criticism of the drive reduction theory of learning is that it does not explain why people engage in behaviors that do not reduce drives. For example, people often eat when they're not hungry or drink when they're not thirsty.

In some cases, people actually participate in activities that increase tension such as sky-diving or bungee jumping. Why would people seek out activities that do nothing to fulfill biological needs and that actually place them in considerable danger? Drive-reduction theory cannot account for such behaviors.

Impact

While Hull's theory has largely fallen out of favor in psychology, it is still worthwhile to understand the effect it had on other psychologists of the time and how it helped contribute to later research in psychology.

In order to fully understand the theories that came after it, it's important for students to grasp the basics of Hull's theory. For example, many of the motivational theories that emerged during the 1950s and 1960s were either based on Hull's original theory or were focused on providing alternatives to the drive-reduction theory.

One great example is Abraham Maslow's famous hierarchy of needs, which emerged as an alternative to Hull's approach.

Reference:

https://www.verywellmind.com/drive-reduction-theory-2795381

CHAPTER EIGHT

Social Development Theory (L. Vygotsky)

Social Development Theory (L. Vygotsky)

Overview:

The major theme of Vygotsky's theoretical framework is that social interaction plays a fundamental role in the development of cognition. Vygotsky (1978) states: "Every function in the child's cultural development appears twice: first, on the social level, and later, on the individual level; first, between people (interpsychological) and then inside the child (intrapsychological). This applies equally to voluntary attention, to logical memory, and to the formation of concepts. All the higher functions originate as actual relationships between individuals." (p57).

A second aspect of Vygotsky's theory is the idea that the potential for cognitive development depends upon the "zone of proximal development" (ZPD): a level of development attained when children engage in social behavior. Full development of the ZPD depends upon full social interaction. The range of skill that can be developed with adult guidance or peer collaboration exceeds what can be attained alone.

Vygotsky's theory was an attempt to explain consciousness as the end product of socialization. For example, in the learning of language, our first utterances with peers or adults are for the purpose of communication but once mastered they become internalized and allow "inner speech".

Vygotsky's theory is complementary to the work of Bandura on social learning and a key component of situated learning theory.

Because Vygotsky's focus was on cognitive development, it is interesting to compare his views with those of Bruner and Piaget .

Scope/Application:

This is a general theory of cognitive development. Most of the original work was done in the context of language learning in children (Vygotsky, 1962), although later applications of the framework have been broader (see Wertsch, 1985).

Example:

Vygotsky (1978, p56) provides the example of pointing a finger. Initially, this behavior begins as a meaningless grasping motion; however, as people react to the gesture, it becomes a movement that has meaning. In particular, the pointing gesture represents an interpersonal connection between individuals.

Principles:

Cognitive development is limited to a certain range at any given age.

Full cognitive development requires social interaction.

References:

- Vygotsky, L.S. (1962). Thought and Language. Cambridge, MA: MIT Press.
- Vygotsky, L.S. (1978). Mind in Society. Cambridge, MA: Harvard University Press.
- https://icebreakerideas.com/learning-theories/

CHAPTER NINE

Motivation:Concept, Types and Motivational Cycle

Introduction

"Motivation"

Motivation is the process that initiates, guides, and maintains goal-oriented behaviors. It is what causes you to act, whether it is getting a glass of water to reduce thirst or reading a book to gain knowledge.

Motivation involves the biological, emotional, social, and cognitive forces that activate behavior. In everyday usage, the term "motivation" is frequently used to describe why a person does something. It is the driving force behind human actions.

Motivation is essential to the operation of organizations and classroom activities. The behavior is caused by the certain causes which relate to person's needs and consequences that results from acts.

Motives are expressions of a person's needs. Incentives on the other hand, are external to the person.

According to Pinder (1984). *"Motivation refers to the forces within a person that affect his or her direction, intensity and persistence of voluntary behavior." According to Lahey (1995), "Motivation is an internal state that activities and gives direction to our thoughts."*

Definitions

According to ***B.F. Skinner****, "Motivation in school learning involves arousing, persisting, sustaining and directing desirable behavior."*

According to ***Woodworth****, "Motivation is the state of the individual which disposes him to certain behavior for seeking goal."*

Motivation doesn't just refer to the factors that activate behaviors; it also involves the factors that direct and maintain these goal-directed actions (though such motives are rarely directly observable). As a result, we often have to infer the reasons why people do the things that they do based on observable behaviors.1

What exactly lies behind the motivations for why we act? Psychologists have proposed different theories of motivation, including drive theory, instinct theory, and humanistic theory (such as Maslow's hierarchy of needs). The reality is that there are many different forces that guide and direct our motivations.

Characteristics

- Personal and internal feeling.
- Art of stimulating someone.
- Produces goal.
- Motivation can be either positive or negative.
- It is system oriented.
- It is a sort of bargaining.

Classification of Motivation:

Primary, Basic or Physiological Needs:

It includes food, water, sleep, sex, etc. These needs arise out of the basic physiology of life and these are important for survival and preservation of species.

Secondary Needs:

They represent needs of the mind and spirit. For example, self-esteem, sense of duty, self-assertion, etc.

Conscious action arises from the needs. Needs create tensions that are modified.

The relation of needs of action is shown below:

- Individual needs (Motives) tensions
- Environment
- Wants (Tension positive negative incentives)
- Perception
- Action (Tension release)

There are three major components of motivation: activation, persistence, and intensity.

- Activation involves the decision to initiate a behavior, such as enrolling in a psychology class.
- Persistence is the continued effort toward a goal even though obstacles may exist. An example of persistence would be taking more psychology courses in order to earn a degree although it requires a significant investment of time, energy, and resources.
- Intensity can be seen in the concentration and vigor that goes into pursuing a goal.4 For example, one student might coast by without much effort, while another student will study regularly, participate in discussions, and take advantage of research opportunities outside of class. The first student lacks intensity, while the second pursues their educational goals with greater intensity.

Sources of Motivation to Learn:

Curiosity

It is a strong motivator of learning. Since, people adapt rather quickly to surprising events, curiosity must be sustained in order to be a continuing source of motivation. To keep the learners alert, instructors can employ such strategies as varying their tone of voice, using relevant humour occasionally, etc.

Learning Task Relevance

Students are more motivated to learn things that are relevant to their interest.

Goal Setting

It is an important source of motivation. When individuals set goals, they determine an external standard, to which they will internally evaluate their present level of performance. Setting goals improves self-motivation and performance to a greater extent. When learners set goals, they seek to gain favorable judgments of their competence or avoid negative judgments of their competence. The recommendation to foster a learning goal orientation runs counter to much current educational practice, which attempts to instill learner confidence within a performance goal orientation.

Motive Matching

It is the degree to which learning tasks meet particular students needs or align with students values. A need can be defined as "any type of deficiency in the human organism or the absence of anything the person requires or thinks he requires for his overall well being." The instructor should be sensitive to individual's needs for achievement and for affiliation.

Self-Efficacy

Motivation also comes from learner's beliefs about themselves. According to **Bandura**, self-efficacy involves a belief that one can produce some behavior, independent of whether one actually can or not. Learners can be sure that certain activities will produce a particular set of outcomes. These expectations are referred as outcome expectations.

Teacher Efficacy

Ashton and Webb (1986) defined **teaching efficacy** as the teacher's judgment about the potential influence of teaching on a child's learning.

Personal teaching efficacy refers to the teacher's judgment of his or her own ability to motivate students.

In other's word, it is quite possible that teachers might believe that teaching has potentially powerful effects on students motivation. but lack confidence that they themselves can affect their own students motivation.

Teachers with high personal efficacy tend to encourage student autonomy and responsibility, structure challenging, learning task and help learners succeed on those tasks.

Types of Motivation

Different types of motivation are frequently described as being either extrinsic or intrinsic:

- **Extrinsic motivations** are those that arise from outside of the individual and often involve rewards such as trophies, money, social recognition, or praise.
- **Intrinsic motivations** are those that arise from within the individual, such as doing a complicated crossword puzzle purely for the personal gratification of solving a problem.

1. Intrinsic Motivation
2. Extrinsic Motivation

Intrinsic and Extrinsic Motivation

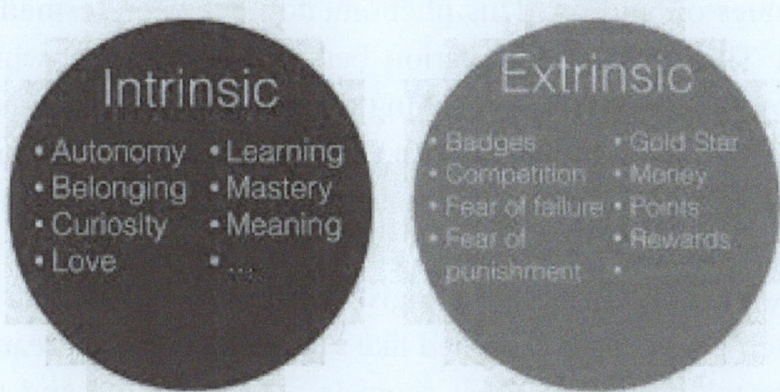

Drives, needs, incentives, fears, goals, social pressure, self-confidence, interest, curiosity, beliefs, values, and expectations are the energizers that direct our behavior.

Some psychologists have explained motivation in terms of personal traits or individual characteristics. Other psychologists see motivation more as a state of a temporary situation. Some explanations of motivation rely on internal, personal factors such as needs, interests, and curiosity. Other explanations point to external factors such as rewards, punishments, social pressure, and so on.

Intrinsic motivation is the natural tendency to seek out and conquer challenges as we pursue personal interests and exercise capabilities. When we are intrinsically motivated, we do not need incentives or punishments because the activity itself is rewarding.

On the other hand, if we do something in order to earn a grade, avoid punishment or for some other reason that has very little to do with the task itself, then it is known as **Extrinsic motivation.**

Recently, the notion of intrinsic and extrinsic motivation as two ends of a continuum has been challenged. An alternative explanation is that just as motivation can include both trait and state factors, it can also include both intrinsic and extrinsic factors. Intrinsic and extrinsic tendencies are two independent possibilities and at any given time, we can be motivated by some of each.

The Cycle of Motivation

The state of motivation is further comprised of four different states, which takes place in an organism to drive him towards each action. Each action is first initiated because of a particular need. The need drives the person into taking actions. Positive results, caused due to the actions, further acts as an incentive motivating a person towards the goal. But the individual can never stop after achieving a certain goal, and this phenomenon continues on and on. This phenomenon has been termed as Motivational Cycle. The cycle of motivation begins with a need, which causes a drive fed by the incentive of reaching the goal that fills the need. But that isn't a cycle; it's a path, a journey with a beginning, middle, and end. A cycle is never ending, like a circle. So why is motivation referred to as a cycle?

Abraham Maslow was the first psychologist to study needs that drive behavior. His hierarchy of needs is designed like a triangle with the greatest needs at the bottom taking up the most room in a person's life and the hardest to reach goals at the top. The process Maslow described showed that humans first and foremost are motivated to survive (food and water). After survival needs are met, they seek safety (shelter that can be protected).

Did you notice what happened? The first need or motivator is survival, but when that need is met, a person does not just stop being motivated. He or she moves on to the next need.

Maslow's whole pyramid of needs is as follows: physiological needs, safety, love and belonging, esteem, and self-actualization. As a person achieves his or her needs in one level, that person moves on to other needs and wants. It is a never-ending cycle.

- **Need**

A need is lack or deficit of some necessity. It's a state of physical deprivation that causes tension within an organism. The tension caused when the organism is deprived of basic necessities of life as food, water, and sleep, causes the internal environment of an organism to be imbalanced. The imbalance caused by the need arouses the organism to maintain its balance. For any goal directed behavior, need is the first condition or stimulating factor.

- **Drive**

Need leads to drive, which is the second step towards achieving goal. Drive can be defined as the state of tension or arousal produced by need. The drive can also be considered as the original source of energy that activates an organism. For instance, when an organism is hungry and/or thirsty, the organism seeks to reduce this drive by eating and/or drinking.

Drive acts as a strong persistent stimulus to push an organism towards its goal. It is the state of heightened tension leading to restless activity and preparatory behavior.

- **Incentive**

The object of the environment that activates, directs, and maintains behavior is called incentive. It can be anything as long as it has either positive or negative value in motivating behavior.

The incentive theory rests on the assumption that the behaving organism is well aware of his actions and the consequences received as a result. The theory also understands incentives as the motivation, which a person has to achieve any particular goal object. The motivated behavior is directed towards incentive and getting closer to the incentive provides satisfaction of the aroused drive.

For example: behavior like eating food is an incentive that reduces the drive of the person caused by the need to fulfill his hunger. The reduction of behavior then cuts off and restores balance in an organism.

According to Hilgard,

The incentive is something in the external environment that satisfies the need and thus reduces the drive through consummative activity.

- **Goal and Reward**

The reduction of tension in the body can be considered as the goal of any motivated behavior. Let's go back to the example of a hungry man. A hungry man eats food, and his body restores to a balanced condition. This then reduces the tension. This reduction of tension as a result of an energized activity is called goal. Once the goal has been completed, the organism is again ready for another goal-motivated behavior.

Goals might be both positive or negative. Positive goals are the ones that an organism tries to attain, such as sexual companionship, food, victory etc. negative goals are the ones that an organism tries to escape from or avoid, such as embarrassing situations, punishments

These four steps continue on and on throughout the life-course of an organism. Because the needs are never ending, it leads to drive, which then lead to incentive and the goal.

For Example: The motivational cycle of the hungry man is over once when he eats and the goal is satisfied. But, the cycle will restart once the man gets hungry again. The cycle goes on and on only to end at the demise of an organism, at which point, the needs permanently stop. Motivational cycle means that behavior goes on in a sequence. Often times, a single motivated behavior can also fulfill multiple needs.

Psychologist now use the concept of need to describe the motivational properties of behavior. A need is a lack or deficit of some necessity. The condition of need leads to drive. A drive is a state of tension or arousal produced by a need. It energizes random activity. When one of the random activity leads to a goal, it reduces the drive, and the organism stops being active. The organism returns to balance state.

References:

- https://benchpartner.com/concept-nature-and-characteristics-of-motivation-and-motivation-cycle

CHAPTER TEN

Theories of Motivation

Theories of Motivation

Introduction

One way of understanding motivation is to look into the theories proposed by psychologist. These theories will help us to understand about instincts, drives, needs, goals and incentives that come under the domain of motivation.

According to instinct theories, people are motivated to behave in certain ways because they are evolutionarily programmed to do so. An example of this in the animal world is seasonal migration. Animals do not learn to migrate to certain places at certain times each year; it is instead an inborn pattern of behavior. Instincts motivate some species to do this.

William James identified a list of human instincts that he believed were essential to survival, including fear, anger, love, shame, and modesty.1 The main problem with this theory is that it did not really explain behavior, it just described it. James presumed that we act on impulse, but that leaves out all the learning/conditioning that informs behavior.

By the 1920s, instinct theories were pushed aside in favor of other motivational theories, but contemporary evolutionary psychologists still study the influence of genetics and heredity on human behavior.

Therefore, we will look into the following four important theories of motivation:

1. Drive Theory
2. Incentive theory
3. Opponent process theory
4. Optimal level theory

Drive Theory of Motivation

The pioneer of drive theory of motivation or 'push theory of motivation' is Freud, who formed psychoanalysis. This theory has the following components:

- **Need:** is a lack or deficit of some necessity
- **Drive:** is a state of arousal and has an elaborate set of driving mechanism along with being instinctive. It takes place by bodily needs or environmental stimuli.
- **Goal directed behavior:** it starts with the drive.
- **Relief:** the reduction of driving state attained with the attainment of a goal.

Therefore, according to this theory, motivation works in a cycle. It starts with a need, which leads to drive and then, moves on to a goal attaining behavior, which leads to successful attainment of goal and thus comes a state of relief.This theory is useful in explaining behaviors that have a strong biological or physiological component, such as hunger or thirst. The problem with the drive theory of motivation is that these behaviors are not always motivated purely by drive, or the state of tension or arousal caused by biological or physiological needs. For example, people often eat even when they are not really hungry.

Incentive Theory of Motivation

Incentive theory of motivation or the pull theory of motivation, applies best to the biological motives (sex, hunger and thirst). According to this theory there is something in goal itself that motivates a person's behavior. The goal which motivates a person's behavior is called an incentive.

For example if you would see a chocolate and rice on a table you would be more tempted to eat chocolate rather than rice because of the certain characteristic that makes chocolate, more desirable. Similarly, when it comes to sexual relations, people get more aroused with ones, they perceive to be sexually desirable. An important point in this theory is that individuals attain pleasure from attainment of positive incentive and by avoiding negative incentive.

Opponent Process Theory

This theory takes the viewpoint of Hedonism. Psychological hedonism, is a concept that believes, humans are psychologically built, in such a way that they only seek pleasure. This theory has some interesting view on what it calls pleasant and unpleasant.

According to this theory an emotional reaction to any stimulus, is followed automatically by an opposite emotional reaction. For example, if a person encounters, a very intense, fearful situation. After some time, he/she would feel calm and composure, even without any change in the situation. Also this theory emphasis that a repeated exposure to a same stimulus may causes an initial reaction to weaken and opposite reaction to strengthen. Therefore, opponent process theory the third law of motion in physics, also applies to the emotions which states that every action produces a reaction.

Optimal Level Theory

Optimal level theory or 'just right theory', believes that human beings seek an 'optimal level' of arousal in their life. Humans neither like to have high level of arousal, nor do they like to have low level of arousal. They just, like to maintain some basic level of arousal. For example, you might have seen a person is in office, doing a lot of work and not answering their phone or text message. This is because, they are trying to reach to their optimal levels. Similarly when a person, feels boredom, they may do some activity to excite themselves. So that they reach their optimal level.

The arousal theory of motivation suggests that people take certain actions to either decrease or increase levels of arousal.

When arousal levels get too low, for example, a person might watch an exciting movie or go for a jog. When arousal levels get too high, on the other hand, a person would probably look for ways to relax, such as meditating or reading a book.

According to this theory, we are motivated to maintain an optimal level of arousal, although this level can vary based on the individual or the situation.

Conclusion

Motivation is the state of mind which pushes all human beings to perform to their highest potential, with good spirits and a positive attitude. The various motivation theories outlined above help us to understand what are the factors that drive motivation. It is a leader's job to ensure that every individual in the team and the organization is motivated, and inspired to perform better than their best. This is neither quick nor easy, but in the long-term, the gains that are derived from happy employees far outweigh the time and effort spent in motivating them!

References

- https://psychologytosafety.com/what-is-motivation-cycle-and-the-4-theories-of-motivation
- https://www.managementnote.com/motivation-cycle/

CHAPTER ELEVEN

Learner's Attitudes In Learning Process

Introduction

It is fact that psychology deals with attitude and characters of learners in learning process. In learning process, it is mandatory for the teacher to know about the learners' personality and his family background for fruitful results from learners in learning process.

Learning of environment plays a significant role in brain development. As, adolescent performs an important mental task. The neural network that supports those abilities strengthen necessary their cognitive, emotion-regulate a memory skills. Without opportunities to use these skills, these networks remain under-developed making it challenging for individuals to engage in higher order thinker as adults. [i] (Robyn Harper, August 2018)

In the materialistic world of mundane life, generally, prefer solution of body requirements rather than development of soul requirements. Every religion and its teachings help us to promote religious and spiritual values that make us civilized and helpful for humanity. Therefore, in learning process, both worldly and spiritual must be fulfilled for the betterment of learners. Otherwise, without spiritual and civilized education, degree may be attained in worldly institutions but the person may be manners-less after neglecting the manners and spiritual teachings of any religion of the world.

There are different types of psychologies but social psychology is that psychology which studies the behavior of mankind. But the requirements of body and soul are different while every man is compound of soul and body. The soul is invisible while body is visible. In societies, there are active and popular organizations on the basis characters of their members or employees or combination of management and members also.[ii] (Masood Tahira Dr., 2017)

Anyhow, behind any person's behavior, there are many factors that influence particular person to adopt strict or soft corner in behavior. In this, past incidents of his life, past accidents of relatives or friends and his current financial position and current friend or relatives attitudes to this particular are also.

As author of 'Social Psychology', stated that behind person's attitudes, past events effect his behavior regarding present thing.[iii] (Mughal Tariq Mahmood, 2013) In the present world, fact is that if any person is deceived by some other person of any other particular tribe or of particular department, definitely, his behavior will be bitter in future on the bases of past events about persons of this particular tribe or department. Similarly, if any learner gets good guidance and feels impressive from any institution, definitely in future, that particular person will have positive views and guides other to get admission in this institution as proposal.

Similarly, in the changing of persons' behaviors, current incidents or losses make persons bitter regarding behavior of the people of societies. [iv] (Mughal Tariq Mahmood, 2013) In societies, if you want spread positive activities then it is necessary that positive values must be encouraged and the persons who are uncivilized, these must be discouraged and their weaknesses must be pinpointed for correction not for discussion.

In educational institutions, generally, teachers' attitude about hard working students and intelligent students remain positive and mostly teachers appreciate these types of learners due to their efficacy in studies. Similarly in any organization, hardworking and efficient worker will be encouraged in the eyes of his boss. Therefore, in educational institutions such types of steps must be taken so that teacher could involve students in teaching activities. In this way, students can become hard working and civilized if regular care is done.

In learning process in schools, the teacher's behavior about the students who complete their work, will be good and favorable rather than those who do not do homework or dull in class activities. [v] (Bhutta Waqar Ahmad, 2009) It is the duty of teachers that they should not neglect the dull students in learning activities so that they can improve their educational weaknesses. It is my practical experience that with proper care, dull and weak students are improved with the passage of time. While if these are neglected and not provided proper care, they leave their studies in early age.

Furthermore, if someone wants to change person's behaviors then by creating difficult situation about future or danger of foreign attack, changing in behavior of the people may occur.[vi] (Mansoor Ali Akbar, 1998) As in the perceptions of war, or danger of war, mostly people will increase shopping than demand due to danger of war. Similarly if educated persons are employed on heavy earnings, this will be encouragement for the present learners to study more on the hope of good paying jobs. If educated persons remain un-employed or can gain low level of income. This will be actually discouragement for present learners so that they will continue study without any interest.

Anyhow, some scholars opine that teachers can correct the behaviors of their students' attitude if they are not doing well. While some others opine that teachers cannot correct students' attitude because they favor of the given quotation, 'Nature cannot change.' Anyhow, changing of students' attitude may be improved in some students while in some students, teachers' guidance may not be improved but for very low number, this may be occurred.

Teachers cannot actually control their students' behavior. That's because the only behavior, person can control in his or her own. And when teachers try directly to restrict what say or do, they are usually left feelings frustrated and helpless. [vii] (Shari Gent, March 22, 2021)

Training of individual is crucial for the promotion of civilized society. In actual, training of individuals in present time will show its results/outcomes in future. This is why, in every department of any country, training is provided for its employees so that particular sense might be developed.

As, Allama Asad wrote that, societies can built only in the result of trainings and polite behaviors of trainers which are used in learning manners. [viii] (Muhammad Asad Allama, March 2009) learners' attitude may be affected from the attitude of teachers or master trainers in learning or training activities. Similarly, if teachers' behavior is impressive then learners will be attracted from his style.

Similarly if teacher will use rude behavior in teaching or in learning activities, this will be dangerous for students and students will feel boredom. Therefore, learning process must be as so that learners feel happy in learning process.

And teachers can control the wrong activities of students in class by presenting such style and manner so that concerning involved student try to avoid from wrong behavior or unsuitable behavior.[ix] (Shari Gent, March 22, 2021) Besides these, if wrong behavior is not corrected by the teacher, or if teachers continue teaching activities and students remain busy in their wrong activities in class, This means both groups are just spending their time, or it may be stated that time is being killed. Therefore, it is better for fruitful results in learning for the students and for the teachers that both should take interest fully. And teachers should perform their duties having fear of God with honestly. Same is upon for learners otherwise there is need to change students attitude regarding learning.

While Edward Kang stated that, teacher can guide students to avoid ineffective studying habits in favor of ones that will increase their learning outcomes. Too often people imagine that long hours of studying are the best path to being a model straight a student. Yet research shows that highly successful students actually spend less time studying than their peers' do-they just study more effectively. [x] (Edward Kang, April 4, 2019)

As concerned the responsibility of teachers or learners concerned, this may be stated that children are innocent so they influence from things and people at once. Therefore, teachers and parents are more responsible as they know the time, the people, about good or bad values and attitudes of the people with their effects. This may supported from Meaning of Holy Prophet's sayings that every child takes his birth in nature but it is upon his parents that make him, Muslim, Jew, Christian or follower of any other religion. The reason is that children are innocents so elders, the old and others are responsible to keep the children on track of success.

And Emma Chippa stated that students are just like agriculture and plants, as you will care the plants safe from any kinds of raw roots or grass, then they will be grow safely otherwise, there will be problem to grow safely and to become civilized[xi]. (Emma Chiappetta, June 18, 2021)

It is empirical evidence that sometimes, educated parents cannot provide better guidance and better learning institution but sometimes uneducated persons can provide better guidance and learning environment. Due to this, the children / learners of uneducated persons can achieve good marks and good values in the societies. This also refers that theoretical values are different from practical values. And for attaining good and civilized values/ manners, adoption of practical values will be useful.

While Edward Kang stated that there are following recommended techniques for high intensity study habits. These are as under:

- Pre-test;
- Spaced practice;

- Self-Quizzing;
- Inter-learning practice;
- Paraphrasing & Reflecting. (Edward Kang, April 4, 2019)

For fruitful learning and better techniques, the learner must involve himself in studying activities. And for preparation of any test, learner must analyze himself by self-test before taking any test so that he can remove mistakes and shortcoming before the actual test time. The advantage of pre-test activities will be useful as it will provide chance to paraphrase the sentences.

In Amin's views, habits become nature when actions are repeated again and again.[xiii] (Muhammad Amin Dr., 2004). In classes, it is duty of teachers and in homes; it is duty of parents that they must know about actions of their young ones so that proper solution for these actions must be proposed.

Without considering this, this habit is useful or not useful, or this habit is good for individuals or for societies. In learning institutions, it is the duty of teacher and management of institutions to provide better conditions for learning activities so that learner can adopt positive and cultured values.

The fact is that sociologists opine that the purpose of social and welfare organizations is to provide satisfaction to humanity regarding their needs. Therefore, mostly organizations are established especially for the promotion of availability of basic needs without considering, caste, creed and color. [xiv] (Bhutta Waqar Ahmad, 2009)

In a comprehensive report about madaris, it is presented that these are spreading mostly positive values besides these, some are promoting particular school of thought which is against unity of Muslim. [xv] (Editor/compiler, 1988) In an analysis about religious madaris of different countries, it is known that religious madaris are more fruitful regarding religious education or for preparation of hereafter life rather than worldly or mundane life of Muslims. But formal and non-formal institutions are preparing just for mundane life rather than hereafter life. Therefore, it may be stated that present scenario, for Muslims, from educational institutions, madaris are more useful than formal schools or colleges or universities only for religious activities and religious education. But the drawback of madaris is that, in this separate school of thought is stressed rather than remain united even within the Muslims. Similarly, in Hindus, or Christians, separate education is provided regarding their religions.

Here, it may be stated that worldly education and the religious education has been divided in different categories among all religion in present era. This is why, educated of one particular school of thought has different point of view about the educated and qualified person of other school of thought or religion. This is the main base of discrimination among the scholars of different institutions in different countries of the world.

It is reality that if you want to know about the level of civilization of any society, or any nation, then from the level of crimes, it may be analyzed that this society or nation is civilized or not. If crimes ratio is low, it refers that people are civilized and these are busy in learning and positive activities.

In Rehman's views those societies promote and become popular in which negative actions and values are discouraged while good values are encouraged by the individuals and by the societies without considering its results. (Rehman Khalid, 2010)

It may be stated from Rehman's views that good qualities and values notify about the level and standard of society. In any society, crimes are increasing and culprits are not sentenced. This refers that in this society, wrong activities are not discouraged or justice system is not working properly. The reason of increasing crime is also easiness and shirking behavior from hardworking. Therefore, such steps must be taken for learners in the institutions so that they could do their work in taking interest and with hard working. Hard working ability will be useful in all the sectors of life in future.

In Saleem's views success is in the hardworking. Those nations become the habitual of hardworking, one day or next day, they can become to see their success.(Khalid saleem Mansoor, 2003) From Saleems' views, it may be stated that from learners' activities, it may be stated that learner will become successful nation in future or not, If the learners of any nation are hard working in their activities, this refers to identify that these learners will soon attain their goal whatever they have set it in their minds. The reason is that it is famous quotation that hardworking is the key to success.

History also shows that great scholars and scientists and great leaders of the world all have common quality/ability i.e. hardworking. With the help of hardworking ability or habit, learners can achieve their goals as intelligent can achieve.

In Shahab's views, as concerned the difference of learning is just like the difference of Muslims' actions.(Shahab Qudratullah, 2004) As concerned Shahab's views, he want say that learning process in different institutions is different because of practical role of teachers/ Muslims. Here, it may be stated that learners are influence from the person they are being provided learning activities. Therefore if a teacher is practical Muslim or practical Hindus or of other religion, then learners will be more attractive from his activities than that person who is not good in his character whether he is a Muslim or Non-Muslim. It may be derived that teacher's role has also influence to the learners. Besides teachers' role, schools/ institutions and management role are not neglect able.

In Monique's point of view, schools can play an important role in adolescents' identity development. No doubt, all adolescents are not same. There are three types of groups of adolescents regarding their abilities.(Monique Verhoeven, Astrid Mita poortuis & Monique Volman, March, 2019) It is fact that the role of schools, colleges or universities may be impressive for learners if its management provide complete facilities to the learners and learning activities are done without wasting time. In this type of institutions, students' knowledge will increase and student will feel satisfaction in the core of their hearts. And these students will become the advertiser of this particular school/college/ university/ institution. Otherwise, student will not consider good about this institution.

Conclusion

In nutshell, it may be stated that learning activities must be impressive for the learners so that it may guide dull and weak learners separately with special care. In learning activities, teachers' role or role of master trainer cannot be ignored. Furthermore, learners' role and their attitude may be changed if some are not taking interest in learning activities. Teachers and the mater trainers also keep in mind that their attitude also must be for the betterment of learners rather than not just for spending time. No doubt, learners' and trainers' attitude regarding values and manners must be ideal otherwise All these activities and trainer's words will not be fruitful for leaners if he is offering words only from mouth rather than core of hearts. Anyhow, with worldly education, religious education must be provided to the learners of particular religion that will create emotions to help humanity. Any teachers/ trainers must keep in mind, the sociological status and economic condition of learners so that they could behave them in light of condition which will be useful in learning process.

References

[i] Robyn Harper (August 2018), "Science of adolescent affect students learning : How body & brain development affect student learning," retrieved

from www.allyed.org, Washington: Alliance for excellent Education, p-1,

[ii] Masood Tahira Dr., (2017) "Why advice is ineffective", Lahore: Monthly periodical Turjuman-ul-quran, p-90.

[iii] Mughal Tariq Mahmood, (2013) " Social Psychology', Lahore: Urdu Science Board, p-206.

[iv] Mughal Tariq Mahmood,(2013) " Social Psychology', Lahore: Urdu Science Board, pp-218-221.

[v] Bhutta Waqar Ahmad," (2009). "Social Work", Lahore: Advanced Publishers, pp-66-67.

[vi] Mansoor Ali Akbar (1998) "Muslim Psychology", Lahore: Feroze Sons,pp-100-1-1.

[vii] Shari Gent, (March 22, 2021) "12 strategies to inspire listening learning and self-control", derived from www. additudemag.com, derived on 16Th July, 2021,p-1.

[viii] Muhammad Asad Allama, (March 2009) " importance of Sunnah", Lahore: Turjuman-ul-Quran, pp-33-34.

[ix] Shari Gent, (March 22, 2021) "12 strategies to inspire listening, learning and self-control", derived from www. additudemag.com, derived on 16Th July, 2021,pp-2-16.

[x] Edward Kang (April 4, 2019)" Research backed studying techniques, derived from www.edutopia.org, derived on 15th July, 2021, p-1.

[xi] Emma Chiappetta (June 18, 2021) "Cultivating Number sense among middle &high school students", derived from www.edutopia.org, pp-1-5.

[xii] Edward Kang (April 4, 2019)" Research backed studying techniques, derived from www.edutopia.org, derived on 15th July, 2021, pp-1-5.

[xiii] Muhammad Amin Dr., (2004) "Islam aor Tazkiya Nafs", Lahore: Urdu Science Board, pp-607-608.

[xiv] Bhutta Waqar Ahmad," (2009). "Social Work", Lahore: Advanced Publishers, pp-64-66.

[xv] Editor, (1988) " A comprehensive report on Madaris' efficacy" Islamabad: Ministry of religious affairs, pp-8-9.

[xvi] Rehman Khalid (2010) " Deeni Madaris, conditions, prospects and problems", Islamabad: Institute of policy studies, pp-17-19.

[xvii] Khalid saleem Mansoor (2003) "Deeni Madaris mey taleem", Islamabad: Institute of policy studies, pp-30-37.

[xviii] Shahab Qudratullah (2004) “Shahab Nama”, Lahore: Sang-e- Meel Publications, pp-230- 240.

[xix] Monique Verhoeven, Astrid Mita poortuis & Monique Volman (March, 2019), “ The role of schools in adolescents identity development, A literature Review, Educational Psychology Review Journal, Vol. 31, issue1, pp-1-2.

CHAPTER TWELVE

Theories of Intelligence

Introduction

Intelligence is the ability to both acquire and apply knowledge and a set of skills required for executing the knowledge from the abstract state to that of practical utility. This involves inculcating an ability to deal with knotty situations, manipulate a difficult environment to human advantage and verify theorems and theories in the realm of objective manifestation of the same. Perception, attention, memory, language and planning are vital preconditions for the successful operability of intelligence in the human domain. Creativity is concerned with inventiveness and originality of invention. Naturally, the creative function requires imagination, ingenuity and vision. Therefore, creativity is a phenomenon by which something of value and utility is formed, at the level of ideation and autonomy. Both intelligence and creativity are significant concerns for effecting a guided visualisation, adaptive performance and brainstorming activity, so that a plan of action takes a material shape, especially if it concerns the learning process.

The study of human intelligence dates back to the late 1800s when Sir Francis Galton (the cousin of Charles Darwin) became one of the first people to study intelligence.

Galton was interested in the concept of a gifted individual, so he created a lab to measure reaction times and other physical characteristics to test his hypothesis that intelligence is a general mental ability that is a produce of biological evolution (hello, Darwin!).

Galton theorized that because quickness and other physical attributes were evolutionarily advantageous, they would also provide a good indication of general mental ability (Jensen, 1982).

Thus, Galton operationalized intelligence as reaction time.

Operationalization is an important process in research that involves defining an unmeasurable phenomenon (such as intelligence) in measurable terms (such as reaction time), allowing the concept to be studied empirically (Crowthre-Heyck, 2005).

Galton's study of intelligence in the laboratory setting and his theorization of the heritability of intelligence paved the way for decades of future research and debate in this field.

Defining the Praxis of Intelligence:

Intelligence is defined as the capacity or ability of a person to acquire information, accommodate and process it and then apply it in appropriate contexts. It is basically that trait that is helpful in managing and facing real life situations. The study of human intelligence dates back to the late 1800s when Sir Francis Galton became one of the first person to study Intelligence. Intelligence aid humans to make decisions, solve problems, formulate logical reasoning, innovate, understand and plan things in the rightful manner and follow a patterned self-awareness with improved levels of motivation and cognitive capabilities. David Wechsler in 1944 defined Intelligence as the aggregate or global capacity of an individual to act purposefully, to think rationally and to deal effectively with his environment. Piaget in 1952 in a similar tone viewed Intelligence as the ability to adapt to one's surroundings.

Factors Contributing to Intelligence:

The most common question which arises is that whether or not there are any particular factors which contributes to intelligence in a person. To understand it, one must know that the combined functioning of a large number of genes generally contributes to Intelligence in a person. Intelligence is also determined to a large extent by the environmental factors surrounding a person. For instance, it has often been noted that a child, with sufficient availability of resources, improved nutrition, proper parenting, tutoring and hailing from a good family backdrop is naturally intelligent and prospers in other major aspects of life.

Concept of Mental Age:

A very close concept associated with Intelligence is Mental Age. It is nothing but a determining factor of how good an individual can utilise his cognitive abilities at a specific age, compared to the average intellectual functioning of a person of his age. While chronological age of a person is based on calendar date as to when that person is born, the mental age of the same person is purely dependent on his or her intellectual development.

For most people, the mental and chronological age are the same and they are said to belong to the average intelligence group. Retarded children have mental ages lower than their chronological age, while gifted children, on the contrary have mental ages higher than the chronological age.

Intelligence Quotient (IQ):

The IQ of a child or adult is normally measured for educational or job placement and is conducted by means of standardised intelligent test. The score of such tests is basically obtained by dividing a person's mental age score (derived from the test) by the person's chronological age, and then multiplying the fraction by hundred. IQ = Mental Age/Chronological Age * 100.

Intelligence, so to say, is a trait which varies from individual to individual, from age to age and from one context to another. Surveys over time have revealed that a majority of people holds average intelligence, a few are very bright and some are very dull.

Theories of Intelligence:

Some researchers argue that intelligence is a general ability, whereas others make the assertion that intelligence comprises specific skills and talents. Psychologists contend that intelligence is genetic, or inherited, and others claim that it is largely influenced by the surrounding environment.

As a result, psychologists have developed several contrasting theories of intelligence as well as individual tests that attempt to measure this very concept.

There are several theories of Intelligence, upholding a concept that is different from the rest. The question which often arises about Intelligence is that whether there is any general intelligence or a multiple set of the same. Opinions have always differed among psychologists regarding this matter and so some of the important theories are discussed below:-

Spearman's Two Factor Theory –

General intelligence, also known as g factor, refers to a general mental ability that, according to Spearman, underlies multiple specific skills, including verbal, spatial, numerical and mechanical.

Charles Spearman, an English psychologist, established the two-factor theory of intelligence back in 1904 (Spearman, 1904). To arrive at this theory, Spearman used a technique known as factor analysis.

Factor analysis is a procedure through which the correlation of related variables are evaluated to find an underlying factor that explains this correlation.

In the case of intelligence, Spearman noticed that those who did well in one area of intelligence tests (for example, mathematics), also did well in other areas (such as distinguishing pitch; Kalat, 2014).

In other words, there was a strong correlation between performing well in math and music, and Spearman then attributed this relationship to a central factor, that of general intelligence (g).

Charles Spearman in 1904 gave his theory that intelligence in a person is typically composed of two factors:-

***G-Factor – which is the inborn ability in an individual and is constant. It is also called the General Ability.**

***S-Factor – which is acquired from the environment surrounding the individual. It is also known as the Specific Ability.**

The aggregate Intelligence that a person possesses is typically the sum total of the G-Factor and the S-Factor, according to Spearman.

Thorndike's Multifactor Theory–

Rejecting the proposition of General ability, Thorndike believed that that individuals require a diverse range of abilities in order to accomplish basic tasks, which he described as Intelligence. He classified the attributes of Intelligence into four categories which are follows:-

a) Level – The toughness or level of difficulty of a task that the individual would be able to solve.

b) Range – Refers to the quantity or number of assignments or tasks that the individual would be able to handle at any given degree of difficulty.

c) Area – The number of proper responses at each level which the individual is capable of giving.

d) Speed – Indicates the promptness with which the individual can respond to the enlisted items.

Thurstone's Group Factor Theory of Intelligence –

Thurstone (1938) challenged the concept of a g-factor. After analyzing data from 56 different tests of mental abilities, he identified a number of primary mental abilities that comprise intelligence, as opposed to one general factor.

The seven primary mental abilities in Thurstone's model are verbal comprehension, verbal fluency, number facility, spatial visualization, perceptual speed, memory, and inductive reasoning (Thurstone, as cited in Sternberg, 2003).

Thurstone believed that Intelligence is a cluster of abilities. Each of these abilities has its own primary factor, thereby contributing a functional unity to the group. Thurstone has basically classified six primary factors, each of which is independent of the others, and they are as follows.

a) The Number Factor (N) – The ability to solve numerical problems with promptness and accuracy.

b) The Verbal Factor (V) – Measured by tests like reading comprehension and vocabulary, this factor involves a person's ability to understand verbal material.

c) The Space Factor (S) – The aptitude of estimating and understanding shapes and patterns typically concerns the Space Factor. For instance, the children's ability to fit together pieces of puzzle to form a coordinated structure, comes under this factor.

d) Memory (M) - It is the cognitive capacity to memorize things quickly with the ability to recall, assimilate and associate previously learned materials.

e) The Word Fluency Factor (W) – Refers to the individual's stock of vocabulary and his sheer ability to think of isolated words with promptness and precision.

f) The Reasoning Factor (R) - The capacity of an individual to decide upon and solve situations with sufficient logic and reason coms under the reasoning factor.

Although Thurstone did not reject Spearman's idea of general intelligence altogether, he instead theorized that intelligence consists of both general ability and a number of specific abilities, paving the way for future research that examined the different forms of intelligence.

Cattell's Theory of Intelligence –

Psychologist Raymond Cattell suggested two forms of Intelligence which are mainly used by pupils in handling problems or situations. They are –

a) Fluid Intelligence – represents intelligence in a human being that is inherited. Fluid Intelligence is mainly helpful in solving puzzles and using problem solving strategies in specific situations.

b) Crystallised Intelligence – that intellectual ability which may not be inherited but obtained through learning and experience over the years. It increases with age and with the prospective years of experience that a person is able to gather in his or her lifetime.

5. Sternberg's Triarchic Theory - Sternberg proposed of three types of Intelligence which pupils normally possesses. They are –

a) Practical Intelligence – The capability of a person to react justifiably in their external environment and behave in successful ways is called Practical

Intelligence.

b) Creative Intelligence – The utilisation of existing knowledge by an individual to carve new methods in handling or coping with problems with a quintessential creative approach comes under Creative Intelligence.

c) Analytical Intelligence – It is the Intelligence which is used by pupils mainly in academic situations. It involves the ability to analyse, evaluate, compare, contrast and react to different aspect of the problem with a degree of precision and is called Analytical Intelligence.

Guildford's Structure of Intellect:

Following the work of Thurstone, American psychologist Howard Gardner built off the idea that there are multiple forms of intelligence.

He proposed that there is no single intelligence, but rather distinct, independent multiple intelligences exist, each representing unique skills and talents relevant to a certain category.

Gardner (1983, 1987) initially proposed seven multiple intelligences: linguistic, logical-mathematical, spatial, musical, bodily-kinesthetic, interpersonal, and intrapersonal, and he has since added naturalist intelligence.

Guildford described Intelligence as a systematic collection of a composite number of abilities which are essential for processing different kinds of information. He used a Factor Analytic technique approach. Guildford believed that an individual's test performance can be traced back to underlying mental abilities or factors which are basically 180 in number and they can be categorized o organised in three broad dimensions: Content, Product and Operations in his 'Structure of Intellect' or SOI Model. The basic dimensions are further classified into several sub categories.

i) Content Dimension – The Content Dimension is divided into four sub categories which are as follows:-

a) Visual – refers to the information which is perceived through seeing whereby the retina forms an image.

b) Auditory – it is the information perceived through learning a piece of verbal information.

c) Symbolic – the information that is read through different symbols or signs representing particular things.

d) Semantic – concerned with information which is verbal or written or even present in one's mind.

e) Behavioural – refers to the information that is perceived through individual acts.

ii) Operations Dimension – The five sub categories of Operations Dimension are as follows:-

a) Cognition- It is the basic awareness of a person involving the general ability to understand and comprehend the meaning of things.

b) Memory – It is the capacity of memorizing and retaining information.

c) Evaluation – It is the judgemental approach of an individual to determine whether a piece of information or answer is constant, valid or reliable.

d) Divergent Production – The process of giving composite or more than one solutions to a single problem.

e) Convergent Production – The process of solving a particular problem with a single and unique solution.

iii)Product Dimension – This is the dimension which applies particular operations to specific contents. Products are further classified into the following six types:-

a) Unit – Concerns with a single item of information.

b) Class – Concerns with a set of items concerning some attributes.

c) Relation – Typically concerns with the connection between items or variables such as associations, sequences, analogies, similarities or opposites.

d) System – Refers to the intricate network of items with their interacting parts.

e) Transformation – It is the change or conversions of perspectives or mutation to an organised form of knowledge. For example- reversing the order of letters to transform it in a word.

f) Implication – Refers to the closure part and is concerned with the inferences, consequences or anticipations of knowledge.

And although this theory has widely captured the attention of the psychology community and greater public, it does have its faults.

There have been few empirical studies that actually test this theory, and this theory does not account for other types of intelligence beyond the ones Gardner lists (Sternberg, 2003).

Howard Gardner's Theory of Multiple Intelligences:

In his book "Frames of Mind: The Theory of Multiple Intelligences", psychologist Howard Gardner suggested that all people have different kind of 'intelligences'. A person, in order to achieve the full range of his or her abilities, cannot just bank on mere intellectual capacity according to him, but rather have to seek help of many kind of intelligences. The utilisation of such intelligences depend on the specific areas on which a particular person is strong and competent. There are nine kind of intelligences enlisted by Gardner all of which are discussed in the following:-

i) Linguistic Intelligence – The sensitivity of a person to perceive spoken and written languages, with the ability to learn and use languages appropriately in the correct context comes under Linguistic Intelligence. People with such intelligences are generally authors or good orators.

ii) Logical-Mathematical intelligence – Refers to the capacity to complete and analyse logical problems, investigate and solve them based on adequate reasoning and the aptitude to carry out mathematical calculations with accuracy and promptness.

iii) Spatial Intelligence – The knowledge about perception of space, whether confined or wide, comes under this category. For example- navigators and pilots have to sense wide spaces and dimensions whereas sculptors or architects have to manage small spaces to give accuracy to their portrayal. Both can be said, thus, to possess spatial intelligence.

iv) Bodily-Kinaesthetic Intelligence – The ability to solve problems by using one's body, parts of the body or mouth or even through unison of mind and body falls under this category.

v) Musical Intelligence – Some people excel overwhelmingly in their musical abilities. They can compose several musical tracks and can perform songs with self-patterned tones or beats. For example, most participants of reality shows in music in the Television comes under this category.

vi)Interpersonal Intelligence – The capacity of an effective interaction or communication with other social members through understanding their choices, desires and intentions is termed as Interpersonal Intelligence. For example, great leaders of the country like Mahatma Gandhi, Jawaharlal Nehru, Swami Vivekananda and other are examples of such.

vii) Intrapersonal intelligence – The most important aspect in an individual's life is self-assessment and understanding by which one should have a clear cut concept of one's own capacities, limitations or strengths. By having a clear perception of one's own self, an individual would not confuse with what he or she himself wants to achieve and do in life and thus can regulate things appropriately. This is called Intrapersonal Intelligence by Gardner.

viii) Naturalist Intelligence – It refers to the conception of the environment in which the individual resides. Some people expertise in the recognition of various species of flora and fauna and loves to be involved in gaining knowledge about them and thus are said to possess Naturalist Intelligence.

ix) Existential Intelligence – This type of intelligence is added by Gardner much laterand refers to some people's knowledge and yearning to handle deep seated existential questions about life and afterlife such as 'Why do we exist?', 'What is the meaning of life?', 'What happens after death?' and so on.

Gardner was of the opinion that individuals can use one intelligence or a combination of two or three intelligences at a time in order to handle life situations depending on his ability or capacity.

Daniel Goleman's Theory of Emotional Intelligence:

It is commonly been noted that there are a large number of pupils who have high IQ and excel in academic life and other facets of life but cannot navigate and understand their own mind and thus fights a conflicting battle with their own self throughout their lives. It is basically at this critical juncture that cognition and emotion should meet and work as a unified whole to develop and facilitate an individual's capacity of reasoning, resilience, empathy, stress management, communication with the outside world and the like. This is called Emotional Intelligence.

John D Mayer and Peter Salovey in 1990 first coined the term 'Emotional Intelligence' and described it as a form of social intelligence involving the ability of a person to regulate one's own feeling and emotions as well as others. In 1990, Daniel Goleman took over the concept and developed his book named 'Emotional Intelligence'.

Emotionally intelligent people can cope up with any crisis situation in a more effective manner than people with less Emotional intelligence. For instance, while an upsetting movie can totally disrupt pupil with less Emotional Intelligence, Emotionally Intelligent pupils seem to be less affected and cope up with the upsetting situation in less time for they have the required logic and reason for handling any kind of situations loaded with discrepancies.

Goleman identified five dimensions of Emotional Intelligence which are as follows:-

Self-Awareness – an individual would first know his or her self properly and identify his or her own strengths or limitations which is the self-awareness of that individual.

Self-regulation – Indicated qualitative restraint and control over one's emotional behaviour and channelize oneself in a proper manner.

Motivation – Emotionally intelligent people are found to be self-motivated and tends to care little about external incentives like money or recognition.

Empathy - The sociability of a person blooms only when he is genuinely empathetic towards the other members of the society and feels for them on a genuine level.

Social Skills – Emotionally intelligent people generally has improved social skillsbased on mutual trust and respect for the other people in the community with whom they live.

Triarchic Theory of Intelligence

Just two years later, in 1985, Robert Sternberg proposed a three-category theory of intelligence, integrating components that were lacking in Gardner's theory. This theory is based on the definition of intelligence as the ability to achieve success based on your personal standards and your sociocultural context.

According to the triarchic theory, intelligence has three aspects: analytical, creative, and practical (Sternberg, 1985).

Analytical intelligence, also referred to as componential intelligence, refers to intelligence that is applied to analyze or evaluate problems and arrive at solutions. This is what a traditional IQ test measure.

Creative intelligence is the ability to go beyond what is given to create novel and interesting ideas. This type of intelligence involves imagination, innovation and problem-solving.

Practical intelligence is the ability that individuals use to solve problems faced in daily life, when a person finds the best fit between themselves and the demands of the environment. Adapting to the demands environment involves either utilizing knowledge gained from experience to purposefully change oneself to suit the environment (adaptation), changing the environment to suit oneself (shaping), or finding a new environment in which to work (selection).

Emotional Intelligence

Emotional Intelligence is the "ability to monitor one's own and other people's emotions, to discriminate between different emotions and label them appropriately, and to use emotional information to guide thinking and behavior" (Salovey and Mayer, 1990).

Emotional intelligence is important in our everyday lives, seeing as we experience one emotion or another nearly every second of our lives. You may not associate emotions and intelligence with one another, but in reality, they are very related.

Emotional intelligence refers to the ability to recognize the meanings of emotions and to reason and problem-solve on the basis of them (Mayer, Caruso, & Salovey, 1999). The four key components of emotional Intelligence are (i) self-awareness, (ii) self-management, (iii) social awareness, and (iv) relationship management.

CHAPTER THIRTEEN

Creativity and Intelligence

Introduction

Intelligence

Intelligence is a broad concept that encompasses many different aspects of cognition. There has been a slew of theories proposed to explain what intelligence is and how it works. Sternberg's triarchic theory of intelligence emphasizes analytical, creative, and practical intelligence, while Gardner's theory claims that intelligence is made up of many variables. Other theories place a strong emphasis on emotional intelligence. A four-and-a-half-year-old child sits at the kitchen table with his father, who is reading him a new story. He begins to turn the page to resume reading, but the child cries, "Wait, Daddy!" before he can do so. "Pig, go! He exclaims, "Go!" as he points to the text on the new page. The father comes to a complete stop and faces his son. "Can you read that?" he asks. The child exclaims, "Yes, Daddy!" "Pig, go! "Go!" he exclaims once more, pointing to the words. This father was not actively teaching his kid to read, despite the boy's numerous questions about letters, words, and symbols that they encountered everywhere: in the car, in the store, on television. The father wanted to see what else his son could understand, so he decided to do an experiment. He scribbled a list of simple words on a sheet of blank paper: mom, dad, dog, bird, bed, truck, car, tree. He put the list in front of the child and asked him to read the words. He read carefully enough to pronounce the words bird and truck correctly. "Mom, dad, dog, bird, bed, truck, car, tree," he said. She inquires, "Did I do it, Daddy?" "Of course, you did! That's incredible." The father gave his son a warm hug and continued reading the pig story, all the while wondering if his son's abilities reflected extraordinary genius or just a normal pattern of linguistic development. Psychologists have wondered what intelligence is and how it might be assessed, much like the father in this story.

Classification of Intelligence

What precisely is intelligence? Researchers have revised their definitions of intelligence countless times since the beginning of psychology. A British psychologist named Charles Spearman believed that intelligence was made up of a single general component called g that could be measured and compared between people. Spearman emphasized the commonalities while downplaying the differences among various intellectual talents. Great thinkers like Aristotle, who lived long before modern psychology, held a similar attitude. Others believe that intelligence is more of a combination of skills than a single factor. In the 1940s, Raymond Cattell proposed a theory of intelligence that divided general intelligence into two categories: crystallized intelligence and fluid intelligence. Crystallized intellect possesses acquired information as well as the ability to regain it. When you learn, remember, and recall information, you use crystallized intelligence. In your education, you constantly display crystallized intelligence by demonstrating that you have mastered the content. Fluid intelligence is defined as the ability to recognize complicated relationships and solve problems. After being detoured into an unknown route owing to road construction, your fluid mind would be required to navigate your way home. Fluid intelligence helps you overcome intricate, abstract challenges in your daily life, whereas crystallized intelligence helps you overcome real, straightforward issues.

Practical intelligence: -

Sternberg's concept of practical intelligence is commonly referred to as "street smarts." Being practical involves utilizing knowledge based on your experiences to discover solutions that work in your daily life. This sort of intelligence appears to be distinct from traditional IQ; people with high practical intelligence scores may or may not have comparable creative and analytical intelligence scores.

The shootings at Virginia Tech demonstrate both high and low practical intelligences. During the incident, one girl left her class to go buy a Coke at an adjacent building. She wanted to return to class, but when she returned to her building after purchasing her drink, she noticed that the exit door had been locked from the inside. Instead of pondering about why there was a chain around the door knobs, she went to her class's window and snuck back inside. She may have thereby exposed herself to the gunman. Thankfully, she was not shot. On the other hand, a few of students were roaming around campus when they heard gunshots nearby. One friend said, "Let's go check it out and see what's going on." "No way," the other student said, “we have to get away from the gunshots.” They did exactly what they said they were going to do. As a result, neither of them sustained any injuries. Although the student who crawled through the window shown considerable ingenuity, he lacked common sense. She’d have a low practical intelligence level. The student who persuaded his friend to run away from gunshots would have much greater practical intelligence.

Analytical intelligence: -

Analytical intelligence is inextricably tied to academic problem solving and computations. According to Sternberg, analytical intelligence is demonstrated by the ability to analyses, appraise, judge, compare, and contrast. It’s customary to investigate the motives of the book’s main characters or research the story’s historical background when reading a classic novel for literature class, for example. In a science course such as anatomy, you must learn how the body uses various minerals in various human systems. To obtain a deeper understanding of this subject, you’re use analytical intelligence. When confronted with a tough math problem, you would employ analytical intelligence to investigate numerous aspects of the problem before tackling it section by section.

Creative intelligence: -

An indication of creative intelligence is coming up with or inventing a solution to a problem or scenario. In this discipline, finding a creative solution to an unexpected problem, creating a beautiful work of art, or writing a well-developed short story are all instances of creativity. Consider yourself camping in the woods with some friends when you realize you’ve left your camp coffee pot at home. The employee who succeeds in preparing coffee for everyone in your company is regarded as having excellent creative intelligence.

Multiple intelligences theory: -

The Multiple Intelligences Theory was developed by Howard Gardner, a Harvard psychologist and Erik Erikson’s former student. Gardner’s idea, which has been improved for more than 30 years, is a more recent advance among intelligence hypotheses. Gardner believes that each person possesses at least eight intelligences. In most cases, a person excels in some of these eight intelligences while failing in others.

Gardner’s concept is still in the works, and additional research is needed to demonstrate its empirical validity. Despite suggestions that Gardner just renamed what other theorists labelled "intelligence," his theories broaden the common definition of intelligence to embrace a larger variety of abilities

"Intelligences" as "cognitive styles" (Morgan, 1996). Furthermore, traditional Gardner intelligence tests are extremely difficult to develop. Emotional intelligence is a term used to describe Gardner's interpersonal and intrapersonal intelligences.

Emotional Intelligence: -

Emotional intelligence is defined as the ability to detect and understand one's own and others' emotions, to display empathy, to interpret social interactions and cues, to manage one's own emotions, and to act in a culturally appropriate manner. Those with high emotional intelligence usually have well-developed social skills. According to Daniel Goleman, author of Emotional Intelligence: Why It Can Matter More Than IQ, emotional intelligence is a better predictor of success than standard intelligence. Emotional intelligence, on the other hand, has sparked a lot of debate, with experts pointing out inconsistencies in how it is defined and depicted, as well as casting doubt on the findings of research on a tough subject to quantify and analyses experimentally.

Intelligence can have diverse meanings and values in different cultures. Knowing how to fish and repair a boat is crucial if you live on a small island where the majority of people get their food through fishing from boats. If you were a fantastic fisherman, your coworkers would most certainly perceive you as intelligent. Your brilliance would undoubtedly be known around the island if you could also mend boats. Consider the customs of your own family.

In some cultures, working together as a group is highly appreciated. In these civilizations, the importance of group achievement outweighs the importance of individual achievement. When you visit a culture, your cultural intelligence, also known as cultural competency, is determined by how well you relate to its ideals.

Creativity

Introduction

Consider all the living beings of earth, they breathe, manage their food, arrange for shelter and reproduce to maintain their generations. Among them, the man enjoys a superior place, they are logical animals, they can differentiate between right and wrong, they can learn the things and they can work to improve their life standards. All these humans are important but the credit of making the life of all human beings better and more comfortable goes to those who have the ability to think differently, to create something new and to do innovations for making the human life easier. James Watt invented the steam engine, William Cullen invented the refrigerator and Martin Cooper invented the mobile phone; all these innovations make the life of humans comfortable but the question arises what ability they possess different from others that make them capable to think in a totally different way? The answeris "Creativity", the ability to think out of the box and find out a new solution to a problem from the available resources.

Someone is said to be creative if they come up with an innovative idea. An example is a creative solution to a difficult problem. But how can you tell if a notion or solution is innovative? Creativity is defined as the ability to conceive, invent, or discover new ideas, solutions, or possibilities. People who are extremely creative frequently have a strong understanding of a subject, work on it for years, contemplate new solutions, seek out the advice and support of other experts, and take risks. Despite the fact that creativity is often associated with the arts, it is a critical type of intelligence that drives people from all areas of life to try new things. Creativity may be found in every facet of life; from the way you decorate your home to a novel way of understanding how a cell works.

Although several definitions of creativity have been given by psychologists, the one most recently derived from the three criteria used by the United States Patent Office to decide whether an invention is patentable is likely the best.

The first criteria are originality. The concept must have a slim likelihood of becoming a reality. In reality, it should be distinguished on a frequent basis. Albert Einstein's special theory of relativity clearly fulfils this condition. There was no other scientist who thought of the idea.

What is Creative Process?

The flow of thoughts and actions that leads to the final shape of an idea is referred to as the creative process. The creative process necessitates critical thinking and problem-solving talents. From musicians to television producers, the five phases that creative people go through to bring their ideas to life are preparation, incubation, illumination, evaluation, and verification. The stages were first articulated by Graham Wallas, a social psychologist and co-founder of the London School of Economics, in his book The Art of Thought, which outlined the essential stages of the creative process.

The 5 stages of the Creative Process

While each artist approaches their work in their own unique way, most artists move through five stages subconsciously while working on their projects. Each of the five stages of the creative process leads to the next in a logical sequence. As you begin your own creative process, relax your mind and allow your ideas to develop through the five stages of creativity.

Preparation stage: -

The initial step of the creative process entails preparation and idea development. This is when you gather information and perform study in order to come up with a novel idea. To develop divergent thinking, brainstorm and allow your thoughts wander, or write in a notebook; this will help you consider all conceivable routes to fleshing out your concept. The first stage of the process involves your brain accessing its memory bank to produce new ideas by drawing on previous information and experiences.

Incubation stage: -

The second stage is to let go of your concept once you've finished actively thinking about it. Taking a step back from your concept before fleshing it out is an important part of creative thinking. You may focus on another project or take a break from the creative process entirely—whatever the case may be, you are not actively working on your idea. While it may appear counterproductive to walk away from your concept, it is a vital step in the process. Your narrative, song, or problem is incubating in the back of your mind during this period.

Illumination stage: -

The lighting stage, often known as the "aha" moment, occurs when the "aha" moment occurs. As new connections emerge spontaneously, the light bulb goes out, and all of the information you've acquired comes together to present the solution to your problem. The answer to your creative quest comes to you in this third step. For example, you can get over writer's block by deciding out your story's ending. It may catch you off guard, but an idea has developed after the incubation period.

Evaluation stage: -

During this stage, you evaluate the feasibility of your proposal and compare it to alternatives. This is also a moment for introspection, as you review your original notion or problem to evaluate if your solution matches your original vision. Market research may be conducted by business professionals to determine the viability of the concept. During this stage, you can either go back to the drawing board or keep going, confident in what you've created.

Verification stage: -

This is when the creative process comes to a close. It's at this point when the real job begins. A physical object, an advertising campaign, a song, a novel, an architectural design—any item or object that you set out to produce, propelled by that initial thought that jumped into your head—could be your creative product. Now it's time to finish your design, bring your concept to life, and share it with the rest of the world.

Role of teacher in foresting creativity

A good classroom setting always includes some creative features, which make learning more engaging and participatory. The perfect combination of creativity and education allows pupils to be imaginative and learn new things. Students can improve their emotional and social abilities while also becoming better communicators. Creative classrooms have the potential to change the way students learn and apply what they learn in the real world. In truth, a student's emotional growth is aided by artistic expression. Let's take a look at how vital creativity is in today's classroom and the benefits it provides.

Learn with fun: -

Students can learn while having a good time in a creative classroom. Teaching methods like storytelling and skits allow students to learn without feeling rushed.

Students are usually up for a good time, and incorporating creative activities into the curriculum increases their enthusiasm for learning.

Teachers should develop this quality in pupils as early as the primary grades, inspiring them to believe in their own inventiveness.

Fun team building exercises can be designed to encourage creative thinking in groups and to teach people how to accept the ideas of others.

Freedom of expression: -

In contrast to traditional teaching approaches, creative classrooms allow them to express themselves. Students get the opportunity to come out of their shells and participate in debates, classroom discussions, and field trips. They feel wonderful and happy because of their freedom of expression.

Contributing to the learning sessions provides them a sense of accomplishment as well. A creative learning technique opens them up to the puzzles that come their way and offers them a sense of accomplishment and pride.

Emotional development: -

A child's emotional development depends on their ability to express themselves creatively. Importantly, this must occur in their lower classes as well, so that they grow up by responding appropriately to events in their environment.

They have the freedom to explore their surroundings and discover new things because of their creativity.

Students will always appreciate a school environment that allows them to explore freely without being restricted. They will gain confidence when they are able to express their actual emotions in a creative manner in their classrooms.

Enhances thinking capability: -

Students' innovative thinking abilities can be stimulated through creativity. In the middle of demanding curriculum schedules, teachers advocate activities such as open-ended questions, creative team building activities, brainstorming sessions, and discussions.

Some teachers utilize these strategies deftly to teach difficult concepts in a way that students like. Puppet performances, for example, will keep students engaged in the learning sessions, and the flow of images in their minds will provide them with the pleasure of creativity. They will be able to come up with inventive replies to the open-ended questions, which will open up a world of imaginative thinking for them.

Reduced stress and anxiety: -

It relieves a lot of tension from pupils when some time is made aside for creativity in between all of the tough study sessions. This joy keeps them relaxed and minimizes their anxiety, allowing them to prepare well for exams and perform well on them.

Including more hands-on learning and allowing for visual reflection will have a significant impact. Encouraging fruitful debates and making the classroom arrangement more adaptable are all important factors in creating a creative learning environment.

Boost's problem-solving skills: -

Children's problem-solving skills can be stimulated through brainstorming sessions using puzzles.

Creativity may drastically affect how students approach an issue, and it can leave them feeling incredibly positive after participating in creative teaching sessions.

In order to help kids, think outside the box and be more inventive and original, creative problem solving can be encouraged in the classroom.

Students will reinterpret the issues or possibilities in this manner, and the answers or replies will be more imaginative.

Improves focus and attention: -

A lower-class child's average attention or concentration span is only a few minutes. Traditional instructional methods would bore them, and they might lose interest in the middle.

Incorporating creative teaching tactics such as storytelling and skits will undoubtedly boost their focus and attention, resulting in more effective study time.

Playing memory games, taking regular breaks and intervals to encourage creativity, and creating a flexible classroom environment will help them enhance their attention span significantly.

Better communication: -

They can improve their attention span greatly by playing memory games, taking regular breaks and intervals to foster creativity, and providing a flexible classroom environment. Classroom arguments not only help children think creatively, but they also help them comprehend and accept the perspectives of others. This type of collaborative creative experience encourages kids to open up and become better communicators.

Follow passion: -

It is critical for a student to pursue their passions in addition to succeeding in academics if they are to be successful in life. A good classroom setting should allow pupils to pursue their interests in music, dance, poetry, sketching, and other forms of art.

This makes kids feel happy, which allows them to approach academics with an open mind.

Setting aside time for such activities can help kids improve their creative abilities as well as their academic abilities. Students who make the best use of these chances can graduate with honors.

Future opportunities: -

Charts that depict the goals, along with timetables, can help students keep track of their progress in a challenging classroom. Students gain the foundation for how successful they can be when they grow up in the school.

The abilities and confidence students develop throughout their school years will have a significant impact on how they progress in their careers.

In reality, those with a creative skill set have an advantage over those with a purely academic skill set in terms of triggering future chances. During the knockout stages, they are allowed to express themselves, and how they show themselves is extremely important in this competitive period.

Innovative mindset: -

Two common creative teaching tactics that help students develop an innovative mentality are open-ended questions and classroom debates. Students are given the opportunity to think critically about the situation or subject at hand and to come up with novel solutions.

The amicable classroom conversations also help kids think critically about other people's ideas and contributions in order to create something new. Lower-class pupils can benefit from a lively classroom environment that is colorful rather than black and white, and teachers might make an attempt to include some comedy in between sessions.

Drive Lifelong Learning: -

A person with a creative mindset has a constant desire to learn new things, which allows them to enjoy the wonderful sense of lifelong learning.

This would keep them interested and busy throughout the day, allowing them to stay young at all times. An inquisitive mind is constantly eager to learn more, and creative classrooms can help children develop a curious attitude in unique ways.

With the rising mobile industry, education apps are on the rise, and there are several fantastic apps that encourage creativity, such as Doodle Buddy, 123D Sculpt, Audacity, and GarageBand.

It is, however, the responsibility of a good teacher to bring the correct mix of creativity into the classroom and to bring out the best in students.

The pleasure of creativity also contributes significantly to improved health, allowing them to continue to flourish academically and in the field of creative.

Some children can sing well without any training, some start dancing well at an early years of age, some can draw the paintings easily and some can solve complex mathematical problems in seconds, each child has some special ability. But some children are totally different from all others. They show extraordinary imagination power, live in fantasies, have variety of unusual thoughts and try to rearrange and create the new toy from their old broken toys. These children are called 'creative children' and their ability to imagine something new is known as creativity. Creativity is the ability to think away from the traditional pattern, to create new ideas and to discover new possibilities. It is actually a kind of intelligence that makes a man capable to innovate something new and valuable. Creative children may combine two or more unrelated words or ideas and give a new answer or novel response to a situation. In a layman's term when an artist create a new painting, a poet composes a poetry and an inventor invents something new; all the creations represent the creativity of their creator and creator through his creation reprsents his unusual and innovative thoughts. Spearman (1931) defined creativity as 'the process of human mind to create new concepts by transforming relations and thereby generating new correlations. 'Stagner & Karwoski (1973) states that 'creativity implies the production of totally or partially novel identity.' Skinner in 1968 postulates that 'creative thinking means that the predictions and/or inferences for the individual are new, original, unusual. The creative thinker is one who explores new areas and makes new observation, new prediction and new inferences.' From these definitions mentioned above it is clear thatcreativity involves creating, inventing or regenerating something new, unusual, unique and useful. It is different from intelligence as it is not limited upto the acceptance and application of knowledge rather it involves divergent thinking, it has originality and its result is something innovative.

Elements of Creativity

Gillford (1986) states that creativity involves divergent thinking which emphasizes on following four components -

1. **Fluency** – Most significant indicator of creativity is plenty of ideas. A normal person when thinks about solving a problem or searches answer to a question, he may find two or three solutions or answers but a creative person can think of many solutions effortlessly.
2. **Flexibility** – Creative people perform divergent thinking. They have plenty of ideas but these ideas are not similar instead creative children have the ability to produce a varied mix of ideas.
3. **Originality** – Creative ideas have uniqueness, novelty and newness. Creative people have the ability to generate new and rare solution to the problem that nobody has listened before.
4. **Elaboration** – The last element of creativity is elaboration. Creative individuals have the ability to elaborate the thought in order to modify or expand upon an idea.

Education and creativity

In his praised talk on Technology, Entertainment and Design (TED), Sir Ken Robinson asked a question: Do schools kill creativity? This has been a much argued issue throughout the history of formal schooling. There are those who maintain that school is actually a place that promotes creativity through arts, music, play and problemsolving in various parts of curriculum and thus advances it rather than extinguishes it. This includes a footnote that many children would never engage in these creative activities unless they were given opportunities to do so in school. Elementary schools have traditionally been places where more creative action and thinking have occurred than in further stages of education.

But then there are those, like Sir Ken Robinson, Seymour Sarason, Shlomo Sharan and Robert Sternberg, who take a more critical stance on that question. Their main argument is that as young people progress through their school education, their genuine interest and innate curiosity in exploring the world around them gradually decline and they seem to be educated out of creativity (Robinson, 2009; Sarason, 1990; Sharan & Chin Tan, 2008; Sternberg, 2006). This happens, they say, because much of what young people do in school is driven by an idea of 'the right answer' and one standard way to get it. The older young people get, the less they have courage to try other ways of thinking and the more they try to avoid being wrong. How much of this is directly due to school and how much it is just a normal course of development remains a disputable issue. Most people connect creativity in schools to subjects that naturally invite one's creative talent to be utilised. Therefore music, visual arts, drama and design are seen as domains that develop students' creative abilities. Rather interestingly, within arts in schools drawing and music are higher in the hierarchy than drama and dance. Therefore it is common in many countries that as the call for more creativity in school education is responded, it means more lesson time for drawing and music. The notion that many more education policymakers and practitioners need to accept is that there are many of us who need to move to be able to think and to create new ideas. Too much deskwork and listening to a teacher is not good for nurturing creativity. As we have shown elsewhere, a vast majority of students' time in school is spent sitting quietly and receiving information from teachers (Sahlberg & Boce, in print).

In our field research we found that in a typical first year upper secondary school lesson there is less than 30 seconds time in total for student-initiated talk. This makes any creative thinking or behaviour in such classrooms practically impossible. Thinking that developing creative thinking and skills is a business of drawing and music in school is, however, a rather narrow view of creativity. If creativity means having original ideas that are useful, it can relate to any activity in school and any subject in curriculum. And it certainly should. Students can engage in creative learn ing in sciences, foreign languages and mathematics, among many others. All teachers can teach almost anything in a creative way so that students need to do things in new ways and come up with novel ideas. But many teachers find this a real challenge for two main reasons: first, many of them think that they are not themselves creative and cannot therefore teach creatively; second, even more teachers think that their own teaching in school should be more creative but they are forced to follow standardised procedures to guarantee that students learn what is included in curricula and textbooks. I will say more about these two points next.

Everyone has some creative talent

If you ask people if they think they are creative persons only very few will answer unconditionally 'yes'. Indeed, most of us think that we do not qualify to be someone who could be named a creative person. I often meet individuals who claim that they are not good at anything. Again, creative people are normally those who paint, sing, dance or invent new things. This is closely linked to a conception that some of have creative talent and most us don't, as Robinson (2009) eloquently describes in his book The Element. Without forcefully challenging this conception it is unlikely that there will be more creative teaching and learning in schools.

If we define creativity in terms of people's artistic abilities we could safely confirm the conventional view that not all have creative talent. What seems to be true with many of us is that we rarely find out in school what our real natural talents are. In other words, we go through our initial education in school without realising what we really can do and where we excel. We find our passion elsewhere afterwards: in our hobbies, through work or in family life. Many people can create unbelievable things that they never thought they could do in school. A number of world known scientists, dancers and thinkers discovered their natural talent only after leaving school. Ex-Beatles Paul McCartney, celebrated choreographer Gillian Lynne and Nobel Prize-winning economist Paul Samuelson are examples of those who think that their schools successfully kept them away from what they really are rather than helping then to discover their true talents (Robinson, 2009). Many of them left school with a belief that they, like most of their peers, had no special creative abilities.

Not the 21st-century education system

Appeal for more creativity and innovation in education comes, not from the education community but from a global economical emergency, technological advancement and the urgent need for change. The main reason is that all national education systems are based on two underlying models: an economic model and an intellectual model. These two systems models are operationally linked to each other. The economic model of education is industrialism that views education as the production of knowledge and skills for predetermined purposes and markets (Robinson, 2009). Teaching and learning are steered by the principles of efficiency and rationalism and are therefore sequenced into manageable units and programmed by a predetermined schedule. The logic of the economic model of education is based on a belief in competition and information as the key drivers of educational improvement — just like they drive efficiency and productivity in market economies. The intellectual model, in turn, views intelligence primarily as an academic ability that is dominated by memory and rote academic skills rather than by broader intellectual, interpersonal or creative processes.

This model assumes that intelligence can and should be measured to determine individuals' educational progress (Sahlberg, 2010). The problem today is that the economic model is outdated and the intellectual model is inadequate for the needs of the unpredictably changing innovation-driven society. Education reforms rarely attempt to challenge seriously these two underlying assumptions of school organisation. Instead, education policies today aim at raising standards, extending time for learning or having more computers in schools. These particular efforts will remain an insufficient means of improving the quality of education unless the basic economic and the intellectual models of education are reconsidered. This has been a long-standing claim by Seymour Sarason (1990), for example, who has predicted that most educational reforms will fail unless the culture of the school will become the locus of change.

Barriers: competition, standardisation, test-based accountability

In many countries teachers have autonomy in their own classrooms to decide how teaching and learning is arranged. Curricula, textbooks and educational guidelines normally stipulate the content and schedule for teaching but methodology is, in most cases, up to a teacher to decide. The emergence of the global educational reform movement, or germ, has brought to many education systems new elements that seem also to regulate how teachers design teaching and learning in their classrooms (Hargreaves

& Shirley, 2009; Sahlberg, 2010). Some of these global trends are particularly interesting and important when creativity and innovation in schools are concerned. Next I will discuss three barriers to more creativity in schools followed by three enablers that might help to reshape teaching and learning in an innovation society.

Barrier 1: Competition as the main driver of educational improvement A particular approach to educational change is based on a belief in competition and information as the key drivers of educational improvement. The logic of this marketorientation is rather straightforward. It is built on the belief that competition — as it does in the market economy — drives efficiency and improvement, and can be applied to schools as well, so that competition among schools would lead to better outcomes for students. In order for schools to compete, individual schools would require much more autonomy. Parents would need to be able to choose the schools their children attended. And finally, in order to choose, parents and the public would require measures of student achievement and education quality to compare and guide their choice of schools, based on a single national curriculum. Competition has forced schools and teachers to look for new aspects in their work. But not so much the way that teachers teach and students learn but rather how schools, districts and entire education systems gain an advantage over other schools in the race for the best students, resources and public reputation. Many schools in England, the United States and even in Finland have recreated their educational profiles. However, the main rationale for doing so is not student learning but competition for resources and better human resources.

Barrier 2: Standardisation of teaching and learning Globalisation has increased competition but also collaboration (Sahlberg, 2006). Both of these lead to coordination and harmonisation of structures and processes. In education this has meant the introduction of standards for teaching, curriculum, expected learning outcomes, school facilities, technologies and so on. Certain compatibility between schools and education systems is required for practical purposes. Standardising teaching and learning through fixed teaching schemes and predetermined learning outcomes is, however, the worst enemy of creativity. There are a number of examples how standardisation negatively affects schools and teaching (Sacks, 2000). When teachers teach by following externally set teaching standards and aim at narrow academic student achievement, they tend not to take risks, try new ways to teach and, thus, be more creative. A good example of an unexpected consequence of standardisation of teaching is diminishing role of collaboration in schools. Individualised testing as an element of standardisation puts personal performance before collective achievement is by definition reducing feeling of interdependency and care in schools. As Sawyer (2007) claims, collaboration is an important condition for creativity and ingenuity.

Barrier 3: Tougher test-based accountability The incentive-based educational reform movement has stimulated enormous debates between and within education and policymaking communities during the last two decades. Holding schools and teachers accountable for students' learning has become a fashionable global movement. Testing and measuring the performance of individuals (both students and teachers), schools, districts and nations have been boosted by the emergence of the educational accountability movement and international student assessments, such as the OECD PISA (Hargreaves & Shirley, 2009; Sahlberg, 2010). The key criterion in this accountability process is the test results determined by external standardised and often multiple-choice tests. According to the emerging evidence, this is leading to narrower curricula, more teacher-centred instruction, rote learning among students and even malpractice and corruption. Each of these, even alone, is damaging for trust, risk-taking and creativity in schools. A critical reviews of these can be found from Wayne Au (2008), Sharon Nichols and David Berliner (2007) and Peter Sacks (2000). School accountability is linked to consequences in the form of rewards such as higher teacher pay or promotion, or in the form of sanctions such as losing one's job or closing down a school. Interestingly, Barack Obama's administration is one of the strong advocates of merit-based pay in the United States. Private tutoring to improve student test scores and thus schools' performance is very common in Egypt, Japan, Korea, and many parts of eastern Europe, just to mention a few examples. Such consequences are certainly not the ways to promote creativity in classrooms. Should creativity be measured in schools? Based on how measurement in general affects teaching and learning the immediate response would be: 'Probably not.' Or at least this needs to be approached with caution. The process of human learning seems to follow much of the similar principles of measurement than measuring simultaneously momentum and place of a moving particle.

Heisenberg's uncertainty principle (1927) says that the measurement of position necessarily disturbs a particle's momentum, and vice versa.

Application: the measurement of creativity necessarily disturbs a student's learning, and vice versa. At least we can conclude that the current culture of measuring students' academic achievements is greatly disturbing both teaching and learning.

The importance of fostering creativity in the classroom

Today's world is changing at an unprecedented rate — and for millions of educators around the world, now may be the single most critical period in history to embrace the benefits and importance of creativity in the classroom.

Looking back 10 years, no one could have predicted the sheer pace of change and the extraordinary circumstances that we'd be facing in today's world — from adapting to the learning needs in the wake of a global pandemic to empowering and building a digital generation capable of starting billion-dollar companies overnight; creativity and abstract thinking have become prerequisites in a student's repertoire of skills needed for the future of society. The last decade alone has seen entire industries completely transformed as a result of globalization and the digital revolution, access to technology and the potential for innovation has never been as accessible as it is today and educators in both physical, and now digital classrooms, play a vital role in fostering and encouraging this creativity.

What is creativity, really?

Creativity in itself is quite a broad subject. While it's easy to look at creativity as a particular skill and assume if you can draw or sing, you must be creative, the reality is far more nuanced. It's fair to say creativity has been the driving force behind the most groundbreaking innovations of our time. When you look around, we're surrounded by innovation that would not have happened were it not for incredibly creative and determined people embracing ambiguity, challenging the status quo, not taking no for an answer and discovering new ways to solve all kinds of problems.

We're living proof that it's nearly impossible to predict the advancements and technologies of tomorrow — from having instant access to the internet from the palm of our hands or having people all around the globe remain connected with a simple click of a button, love it or loathe it, the advancements we've made in technology affect almost everything we do today. It also influences most of our plans for the future, and yet what we take for granted today — TV streaming, GPS in our cars, libraries of content from all over the globe and online shopping — were not the norm, or so seamlessly integrated into our everyday life a decade ago.

The role and importance of creativity in the classroom

To find out more about the importance of nurturing creativity in the classroom, I spoke with Amber Kemp-Gerstel, a clinical child psychologist come modern day 'Art Attack', content creative and TV personality with more than a decade of experience in creative therapy. Our conversation shed some light on the role and importance of creativity in a classroom, with Amber explaining a classroom environment is one of the most important places to start encouraging and nurturing creativity in young people.

As adults, it can be easy to get caught up in the day-to-day and let the guardrails of society stunt our ability to think abstractly and pursue bold ideas that contradict the 'norm'. Conversely, children are best-positioned to develop their ways of thinking and solving problems as they are naturally inquisitive, open to learning, imaginative and they do not often feel embarrassed by novelty, since everything is new and consequently nothing is really abnormal. Generally speaking, with some teachers spending over 10,000 hours in a child's life as they progress from kinder to high school, it's crucial they nurture this behaviour and near limitless thinking, further support and encourage it as it plays an important role in developing the soft skills needed in life outside of the classroom.

In addition, the late Sir Ken Robinson was also vocal on the importance of interweaving creativity into the education system, stating education "takes us into a future we can't grasp", and thus creativity is imperative to overcoming blockers or challenges in the future.

Assessing the creative process

Psychometric measures of creative process and potential has been extensively implied in the field. These processes involve cognitive factors that lead to creative production like finding and solving problems, selective encoding (i.e. selecting info that is relevant to problem and ignoring distractions), evaluation of ideas, associative thinking, flexibility and divergent thinking. Nevertheless, from this long list of cognitive factors the assessment of creative process mostly relied on divergent thinking in the creativity assessment tests. Even researchers in Ref. [24] underlined the irony in the study of creativity, although creativity itself requires novel and original solutions to a problem, researchers mostly focused on divergent thinking (DT) tasks. Not only major efforts were put on developing DT tests, even the earliest DT tests are still widely used in creativity research and educational areas. Divergent thinking can be explained as a thought process used to generate creative ideas via searching for many possible solutions. Whereas, convergent thinking is the ability to arrive the "correct" solution. Guilford [25] who came up with these concepts clearly underlined the difference between them.

In convergent thinking tests, the examinee must arrive at one right answer. The information given generally is sufficiently structured so that there is only one right answer... An example with verbal material would be: "What is the opposite of hard?" In divergent thinking, the thinker must do much searching around, and often a number of answers will do or are wanted. If you ask the examinee to name all the things, he can think of that are hard, also edible, also white, he has a whole class of things that might do. It is in the divergent thinking category that we find the abilities that are most significant in creative thinking and invention.

In divergent thinking it is important to produce as many responses to verbal or figural stimuli as possible such that, more is better in DT. After the examinee come up with various answers, testers score them. The scoring is based on the concepts of originality (uniqueness of responses to a given stimuli), fluency (number of responses produced to a given stimuli), flexibility (number and/or uniqueness of categories of responses to a given stimuli) and elaboration (to add details to the ideas produced for a given stimuli) . As Guilford pioneered the research on creativity, initial efforts to assess it came from him and his colleagues too. Though, there were others who developed test batteries to measure creative thinking abilities and focused mostly on process components (e.g., Kogan and Wallach, Torrance, Mednick).

Structure of Intellect Divergent Thinking Test: Guilford's famous Structure of Intellect Model (SOI) was mainly about defining and analyzing the factors constitute intelligence and he proposed 24 distinct types of DT. His model covers 180 (6x5x5) intellectual abilities organized along three dimensions namely; operations (evaluation, convergent production, divergent production, memory, cognition), contents (visual, auditory, symbolic, semantic, behavioral) and products (units, classes, relations, systems, transformation, implications). Guilford's SOI battery included several DT tasks like; in figural implications examinees were required to add lines to simple figures to create a new figure or in semantic units, listing commonly mentioned consequences of an impossible event, such as people not needing to sleep. Other examples include the Making Objects task (fluency with figural systems); in which participants make a new object from the provided four and by using alt least two of them or the Name Grouping task (flexibility with symbolic classes) which requires participants, given a set of names, forming subgroups based on different rules.

"Guilfordian" Tests: Guilford's work was so influential that it was followed, replicated and reinterpreted by different researchers in 60s. Wallach and Kogan argued that creativity tests should be administered in a game-like environment and should not apply time limitations. With this in mind, they focused on assessing creativity in children and developed the Instances Test (list as many things that move wheels, things that make noise) and the Uses Test (tell me the different ways you can use knife, tire or like in Ref. toothpicks, chair or bricks). Wallach and Kogan proposed a different perspective than Guilford, not in the content of the test but for the target age group and way of administration (for a detailed discussion on the effects of different testing environments see reference [30]). Testing the divergent thinking ability of children would allow the educators and educational institutions to recognize their creatively able children and provide the necessary support and enrichment in their education.

Torrance Tests of Creative Thinking (TTCT): If we were to make a hits list for creativity assessment tests, TTCT most probably would be the number one. Torrance's name was equated with assessment of creativity but it was not his major goal. TTCT was developed for research and to provide a tool that can be used to individualize the instruction . The TTCT, which are mainly based on SOI battery, are the most widely used and studied creativity tests and continue to attract attention in international level . Over the course of years, TTCT was refined in terms of scoring and administration and re-normed, which can account for its popularity. The TTCT consist of two different tests, the TTCT-Verbal and the TTCT-Figural, and each test has two parallel forms allowing it to be used as pre-posttests in experimental settings. The TTCT scores were expressed by four factors: fluency, originality, flexibility and elaboration. After the streamlined system introduced, Figural tests scored for resistance to premature closure and abstractness of titles in addition to originality, fluency and elaboration. Flexibility was removed because of the close correlation between fluency and flexibility scores . The TTCT recommend an administration of game-like environment like Wallach and Kogan but apply time limitations.

The TTCT-Verbal is entitled as "Thinking Creatively with Words" and the Figural form entitled as "Thinking Creatively with Pictures". Verbal form consists of six activities each whereas figural form consists of three

Conclusion

Creativity is the ability to think differently. It is a quality of an individual that is less ordinary. Creativity enables to think out of the box and construct wonder from waste. Some learners are born with this precious quality and some develop it through the experiences. Creativity is the foundation of innovation and inventions. Creative children are not only divergent thinkers but also unique creators. Most of the existing crisis can be resolved through creative approach. Creativity is the cherished virtue that separates the learners and provides a special identity. It eases the path of personal and social life of the learners. We need to identify and acknowledge such children who have creative instincts and the ability to think beyond. Their creativity should be recognised and promoted. Creativity is the solution to various complex issues and problems. It is the origin of innovation and invention. These innovations and inventions reduce the human efforts and enhance efficiency, utility and production. Therefore, it can be concluded that creativity resolves human issues and eases human efforts and optimises the outcomes. We need to foster creative instincts, temper and thinking in the learners from the beginning to help them use their full potential and skills.

Embracing creativity in the classroom is a great way to challenge the notion of static learning: the idea that there's merely one correct way to solve a problem or come to a solution. Whilst one plus one will always equal two, there are a multitude of ways to teach that concept. The advent of the internet and the omnipresence of connected devices has opened up new opportunities for people of all ages to have instant access to new information and different ways of thinking and doing things.

We know not everything always goes to plan the first time around, so it's critical to encourage young people to acknowledge this and find alternative and unique solutions to the challenges at hand, meanwhile building resilience and confidence in their ability.

All in all, creativity has become a prerequisite for innovation and will be an increasingly in-demand skill for jobs of the future. Creativity doesn't need to be a subject of its own, instead, it should be weaved into absolutely every aspect of learning and teaching.

CHAPTER FOURTEEN

Personality and Adjustment

Introduction:

Personality is the product of social interaction in group life. In society every person has different traits such as skin, color, height and weight. They have different types of personalities because individuals are not alike. It refers to the habits, attitudes as well as physical traits of a person which are not same but have vary from group to group and society to society, everyone has personality, which may be good or bad, impressive or unimpressive. It develops during the process of socialization in a culture of a specific group or society. One cannot determine it of an individual exactly because it varies from culture to culture and time to time. For example, a killer is considered criminal in peace time and hero in war. The feeling and actions of an individual during interaction moulds the personality. It is the sum of total behaviors of the individual and covers both overt and covert behaviors, interests, mentality and intelligence. It is the sum of physical and mental abilities and capabilities.

Personality has been derived from the Latin word "persona" which means "mask" used by the actors to change their appearance. It is the combination of an individual thoughts, characteristics, behaviors, attitude, idea and habits.

Definition of Personality:

Macionis define as "It is the constant pattern of thinking, feeling and acting."

Ogburn and Nimkoff define it as the totality of sentiments, attitudes, idea, habits, skills and behaviors of an individual."

Trait-based personality theories, such as those defined by Raymond Cattell, define personality as the traits that predict a person's behavior.

Brinkerhoff defines personality as the unique attributes and abilities of the individual.

Dewy and Humber look at personality as the way by which the individual is interrelated through ideas, actions, and attitudes to the many non- human aspects of his/her environment and biological heritage.

- *Personality defines as the structures inside a person that explain why he or she creates a particular impression on others (MacKinnon, 1969).*
- *Personality defines as a stable set of characteristics and tendencies that determine commonalities and diff*erences in people's behavior (James, 1994).

Personality Concept

Personality refers to a person's mental and physical well-being.

personality, a characteristic way of thinking, feeling, and acting. personality embraces temperaments, perspectives, and sentiments and is most obviously communicated in connections with others. It incorporates conduct attributes, both intrinsic and obtained, that recognize one individual from one more and that can be seen in individuals' relations to the climate and to the gathering.

The term personality has been characterized in numerous ways, yet as a mental idea two principal implications have developed.

The first relates to the steady distinctions that exist between individuals: in this sense, the investigation of character centers around arranging and making sense of somewhat stable human mental attributes.

The subsequent significance stresses those characteristics that make all individuals the same and that recognize mental man from different species; it guides the character scholar to look for those consistencies among all individuals that characterize the idea of man as well as the elements that impact the course of lives. This duality might assist with making sense of the two bearings that personality studies have taken: from one viewpoint, the investigation of perpetually unambiguous characteristics in individuals, and, on the other, the quest for the coordinated entirety of mental capacities that accentuates the interchange among natural and mental occasions inside individuals and those social and organic occasions that encompass them. The double meaning of personality is interlaced in a large portion of the themes examined beneath. It ought to be accentuated, notwithstanding, that no meaning of personality has tracked down widespread acknowledgment inside the field.

Davidson writes on temperament, that is socially developed once having a genetic base, through time in his medical textbook, "Principles and observe of drugs." once passing through a succession of biological process stages, the individual reaches associate adult psychological stage.

“Personality is that the most applicable conceptualisation of a person’s behaviour with all its characteristics, that the soul will offer in an exceedingly moment,” McClelland says.

According to Davidson’s conception, there area unit three completely different parts of one’s temperament and its development and growth: social, physiological, and psychological. McClelland has targeted on the psychological factors that influence desired changes in {an individual’s|a person’s|a temperament’s|a human|somebody’s} behaviour and personality.

As a result, each of those ideas shed some light-weight on the formation of temperament and individual behaviour. excluding Allport’s comprehensive approach to the topic, each of those definitions have the foremost application and utility in organisational behaviour.

An individual’s temperament is exclusive, personal, and a primary issue of his behaviour.

Individuals answer completely different events in several ways that thanks to variances in temperament. Some temperament theorists highlight the necessity of recognising the person-situation interaction, i.e., personality’s social learning parts. The study of human behaviour would profit greatly from such associate interpretation.

Characteristics of Personality:

You’ll be asked to list your personal attributes if you apply for employment. Employers assume that your temperament is very fastened and will not vary considerably from year to year. whereas most folks will relate to the current notion, wherever will our temperament originate? Is it in our polymer, or is it additional a results of our formative circumstances?

The answer is, of course, both. as a result of our brain and therefore the chemicals that act inside it area unit generated by genes, there area unit bound to be genes that influence our behaviour. Finding anybody of the many genes concerned, on the opposite hand, is notoriously tough. as a result of personalities area unit complicated, the biology of behaviour is as complicated.

Scientists area unit solely currently commencing to gain a more robust understanding of however genes have an effect on behaviour.

i. Temperament is well-structured and consistent.

ii. Temperament may be a psychological attribute that's influenced by biological processes and necessities.

iii. Temperament influences however folks behave.

iv. Temperament is expressed in an exceedingly kind of ways that, together with thoughts, feelings, and behaviours.

The word personality itself stems from the Latin word persona, which refers to a theatrical mask worn by performers in order to either project different roles or disguise their identities. At its most basic, personality is the characteristic patterns of thoughts, feelings, and behaviors that make a person unique. It is believed that personality arises from within the individual and remains fairly consistent throughout life. The important roles as well as the following fundamental characteristics of personality:

- **Consistency:** There is generally a recognizable order and regularity to behaviors. Essentially, people act in the same ways or similar ways in a variety of situations.
- **Psychological and physiological:** Personality is a psychological construct, but research suggests that it is also influenced by biological processes and needs.
- **Behaviors and actions:** Personality not only influences how we move and respond in our environment, but it also causes us to act in certain ways.
- **Multiple expressions:** Personality is displayed in more than just behavior. It can also be seen in our thoughts, feelings, close relationships, and other social interactions.

Types of Personality:

Personality is those qualities through which you present yourself in front of others, these are such qualities that decide your reaction on an action of a person. It covers everything of an individual, for example walking, talking, treating and handling problems. It is a tool that measures the confidence of an individual. There are three types of personalities explained by sociologist they are:-

- **Entrovert**
- **Introvert**
- **Ambivert**

1. Extrovert Personality:

This type has the tendency to live mostly outside the like to live with others. Those individuals are highly socialized and have contact with outside people in the society. They want to join other groups who are more in number. These type of people are drivers, excessive drinkers, smokers, robbers, thieves, wicked persons etc.

2. Introvert Personality:

Introvert is opposite to extrovert. Those people are always live alone in their rooms and do not want to go outside. They have their own imaginary world. They are teachers, scientists, thinkers and philosophers.

3. Ambivert Personality:

Between extrovert and introvert personalities there is a third one type called ambivert. People belonging to this type enjoy both the groups and attend them. They have middle mind and want to live in both parties. Sometimes they join outside people but sometimes they live in their own rooms.

Understanding the four different personality types

It's important to understand that everyone can be categorised based on the behaviour and personality traits they exhibit. There are lots of different personality tests that one can undertake but the one we are going to concentrate on is the personality type A, B, C and D.

In these personality types, anyone can be grouped into the four categories, however, they are not exclusively grouped into just one category or type. That is because everyone will exhibit more dominant personality traits from one of the types but have elements from another.

These personality types can be used to understand a job candidate's personality among other things. From identifying people who are more likely to be a better team player, to those with characteristics set to lead, hiring managers can use these personality tests to create a team which has a more balanced environment and even improve staff retention.

As discussed, the tests are indicators into personality type, and cannot put you firmly in one category or another. There will be more dominant traits in each category type but it is rare to find people who just fit the mould of one.

We will now take a closer look at the different personality types and highlight some of the more key attributes to each letter.

Type A personality

The Type A personality is the "go getter" type. They have very high standards, are extremely competitive, love to set goals and they love to achieve as many as possible.

However, the type A personality will struggle not so much when things are going wrong, but when things are going right. Even if the outcome is positive or very good, they want to do it again because they think it can be done better.

The Type A personality can also be known as, Director.

Goal orientated, risk taker and good under stress the Type A personality will show themselves to be incredibly diligent and hardworking employees and leaders. Sometimes, too hard working with workaholic tendencies, staying as long as possible to make sure the job gets done to the exacting standards they hold. Better left working alone rather than in teams, being restricted will have significant adverse effects.

You will see many Type A personalities in senior leadership positions - or trying to get there - and even in entrepreneurship roles.

Type B personality

The Type B personality is the laid back one. These are people who are generally very grounded and peaceful in their demeanour.

Don't however think that this is someone who is very placid. On the contrary, they love being around people and love being the centre of attention. Their driving need is to be liked by pretty much everyone. Being applauded or acknowledged is key to their personality.

The Type B personality can also be known as, Socialiser.

Relationship orientated, outgoing and enthusiastic, the Type B personality will be someone who loves to talk about themselves - not to show off - but to be liked. Being well turned out and knowledgeable about many things is a driving factor for them. Any form of public humiliation is, however, devastating as it is seen as an attack on the whole person, rather than just the isolated situation.

At work, they would be the relationship builders, the ones who could cultivate better working environments with different personalities and are very good at turning ideas into workable solutions.

Type C personality

The Type C personality is the detailed one. They thrive in environments where their things are controlled and stable.

Being accurate, rational and applying logic to everything they do is where this personality really shows itself. Demanding logic over emotion is a natural dominant feature. Not suffering from hype or drama, in fact, they dislike it because they want facts and data.

The Type C personality can also be known as the Thinker.

Detail orientated, logical and prepared, this careful, resourceful and thinking personality is very good in a situation where everything needs to be analysed before any stands are taken. They like to control everything, even others which can be a negative aspect of this personality. Having all the facts at hand makes them a very difficult person to break down in opposing ideas or questioning as they interpret everything with the information they have and are given.

In a working environment, they are meticulous with the information and the data that they have to hand. You will commonly see Type C personalities in roles within science, medicine and law.

Type D personality

The Type D personality is the existentialist one. They are calm on the surface and enjoy things to remain the same as long as possible.

Hard working in nature, they are people pleasers like Type B but want to know that they are needed for their work rather than being validated over just who they are. They require a sense of security and believe that taking risks or change is actually quite dangerous and imposing on life balance.

The Type D personality can also be known as the Supporter.

Task orientated, stabilising and cautious, this very organised personality is someone who is seen as a supporter within a business. A supporter in the sense of helping others, showing compassion, thoughtfulness and caring. They need to feel part of a team, but in that team they can act as a paternal figure, helping others to achieve and never giving up on the task or the business.

In a working environment they are very good at delivering repetitive tasks - in fact, they enjoy that lack of variety because change can cause distress. They are also very good with attention to detail, making them a desirable candidate who requires stability in their role.

The most effective method to test for the 4 character types

A workplace personality test is a basic appraisal that utilizes generally acknowledged mental speculations to assist with acquiring a far-reaching understanding into an individual's reasonableness to a job. This will take a gander at things, for example, receptiveness to change, how they manage pressure, how aggressive they may be and so on.

By giving the business an elevated degree of definite knowledge on their representatives, they will actually want to recognize who falls into every one of the character types. There are likenesses and shared attributes across the four character types, just with the extra knowledge from a character test will it become clear which clients fall into each kind.

Thomas gives an extensive personality test to estimate individual characteristics and how they connect with the work environment.

How Thomas appraisals measure work environment character

Thomas' working environment personality test can be utilized to help evaluate and comprehend an applicants or representative'spersonality test and more extensive character.

In light of the around the world perceived and regarded 'Enormous 5' mental hypothesis, the High Potential Trait Indicator (or HPTI) as we additionally call it, evaluates six center attributes (Conscientiousness, Adjustment, Curiosity, Risk Approach, Ambiguity Acceptance and Competitiveness) to assist you with distinguishing the best possibility for a job and recognize authority potential, adding certainty to your enrollment.

Whether you are Type An or Type C, it is feasible to comprehend that we as a whole have various approaches to connecting with our current circumstance and individuals that we work with. We are every one of the a combination of various character types however with additional predominant aspects from one over the other. Having a grip of the more predominant aspects prompts a superior comprehension of the sort of individuals we work with and the sort of individuals we are.

The four character types include:

Normal: The most well-known type are individuals who are high in neuroticism and extraversion while lower in receptiveness.

Reserved: People in this sort are not open or hypochondriac however they are sincerely steady. They will generally be thoughtful, pleasant and honest.

Role-models: These individuals are normal pioneers with low degrees of neuroticism and elevated degrees of pleasantness, extraversion, transparency and uprightness. They pay attention to novel thoughts and are dependable.

Self-centered: While these individuals score high in extraversion they rank sub optimal transparency, suitability and uprightness.

"The way for you to develop is to be familiar with yourself," Amaral said.

Personality Nature

Every person's temperament is expounded to his or her nature. In general, someone asserts himself by his temperament traits. With their years of expertise, mature folks adopt associate objective perspective toward themselves et al.. They conjointly mirror on themselves so as to reinforce their temperament and behavior.

i. Self-Consciousness:

People at large and alternative species area unit immensely completely different. His temperament is marked by a attribute notable as'self-consciousness,' that permits him to remember of his surroundings and self-identity.

ii. Atmosphere Adaptability:

Off and on, temperament will build diversifications in response to desired changes. The term "resistance to change" refers to a disagreement defined by tension and conflict. folks sometimes comply with new surroundings and obstacles. Adaptation to new settings is usually in the middle of a modification in behaviour pattern, leading to a sleek operating condition and a nice atmosphere.

iii. Goal-oriented:

Folks try and accomplish their objectives. people do have the motivation to realize their objectives. Motive is that the results of needs and necessities. a person's want leads his or her behaviour toward achieving that want. activity changes area unit influenced by each physiological and social factors.

iv. Temperament Integration:

temperament works in an exceedingly consistent manner by combining varied activities (both mental and private experiences). temperament comes in an exceedingly kind of shapes and sizes. temperament is differentiated by the style within which it's integrated. folks with developed personalities have a powerful association to their values and experiences. this can be determined by their activity standards, that they need developed from childhood.

Who Were the Neo-Freudians?

Many of the most tenets of Freud's psychotherapy theory were given by Neo-Freudian psychologists, however they updated and tailored the approach to accommodate their own beliefs, thoughts, and opinions. scientist brain doctor instructed a spread of polemic views, however he conjointly noninheritable an oversized following.

Many of those students united with Freud's ideas regarding the unconscious and therefore the importance of childhood development. alternative students, on the opposite hand, disagreed or outright rejected variety of things. As a result, these people developed their own distinct conceptions of temperament and psychological feature.

Neo-Freudian Disagreements

These neo-Freudian thinkers disagreed with neurologist for a spread of reasons. Erik Erikson, as an example, argued that brain doctor was mistaken in basic cognitive process that childhood events affected temperament virtually entirely. alternative considerations that role player neo-Freudian philosophers' attention were:

The importance of sexual needs as a basic motive in Freud's theory

The absence of social and cultural influences on behaviour and temperament in Freud's work

Sigmund Freud's demoralised read on attribute

Many neo-Freudians believed that Freud's theories were too targeted on psychopathology, sex, and childhood events.

Instead, several of them selected to focus their theories on a lot of positive aspects of attribute moreover because the social influences that contribute to temperament and behavior.1

While the neo-Freudians might are influenced by Freud, they developed their own distinctive theories and views on human development, temperament, and behavior.

Major Neo-Freudian Thinkers

There were variety of neo-Freudian thinkers World Health Organization stone-broke with the brain doctor psychotherapy tradition to develop their own psychodynamic theories. a number of these people were at first a part of Freud's set, as well as Carl Jung and male monarch Adler.

Carl Jung

Carl Jung and Freud once had an in depth relationship, however Carl Gustav Jung stone-broke away to make his own concepts.2 Carl Gustav Jung observed his theory of temperament as analytical scientific discipline, and he introduced the conception of the collective unconscious. He delineated this as a universal structure shared by all members of an equivalent species containing all of the instincts and archetypes that influence human behavior.

Jung still placed nice stress on the unconscious, however his theory placed a better stress on his conception of the collective unconscious instead of the private unconscious. Like several of the opposite neo-Freudians, Carl Gustav Jung conjointly centered less on sex than Freud did in his work.

Alfred Adler

Alfred Adler believed that Freud's theories centered too heavily on sex because the primary incentive for human behavior.3 Instead, Adler placed a lesser stress on the role of the unconscious and a larger target social and social influences.

His approach, called individual scientific discipline, was focused on the drive that each one folks need to complete their feelings of inferiority. The complex, he urged, was somebody's feelings and doubts that they are doing not qualify to people or to society's expectations.4

Erik Erikson

While Freud believed that temperament was largely set in stone throughout time of life, Erikson felt that development continuing throughout life. He conjointly believed that not all conflicts were unconscious. He thought several were aware and resulted from the method|biological process} process itself.

Erikson de-emphasized the role of sex as a incentive for behavior and instead placed a far stronger target the role of social relationships.

His eight-stage theory of psychosocial development concentrates on a series of biological process conflicts that occur throughout the period of time, from birth till death. At every stage, folks face a crisis that has got to be resolved to develop sure psychological strengths.5

Karen Horney

Karen Horney was one amongst the primary girls trained in psychotherapy, and she or he was conjointly one amongst the primary to criticize Freud's depictions of ladies as inferior to men. Horney objected to Freud's portrayal of ladies as full of "penis envy."

Instead, she steered that men expertise "womb envy" as a result of they're unable involved youngsters. Her theory focuses on however behavior was influenced by variety of various neurotic desires.

Trait Theories of Personalities

Trait theorists believe temperament are often understood by positing that every one individuals have sure traits, or characteristic ways in which of behaving. does one tend to be sociable or shy? Passive or aggressive? Optimistic or pessimistic? in keeping with the Diagnostic and applied mathematics Manual (DSM) of the yank medicine Association, temperament traits ar outstanding aspects of temperament that ar exhibited in an exceedingly wide selection of necessary social and private contexts. In alternative words, people have sure characteristics that partially confirm their behavior; these traits ar trends in behavior or angle that tend to be gift in spite of matters.

An example of a attribute is extraversion–introversion. sociableness tends to be manifested in outgoing, talkative, energetic behavior, whereas introversion is manifested in additional reserved and solitary behavior. a personal might fall on any purpose within the time, and therefore the location wherever the individual falls can confirm however he or she responds to varied things.

The idea of categorizing individuals by traits are often derived back as so much as Hippocrates; but additional fashionable theories have come back from Gordon Allport, Raymond Cattell, and Hans Eysenck.

Gordon Allport (1897–1967)

Gordon Allport was one amongst the primary fashionable attribute theorists. Allport and Henry Odbert worked through 2 of the foremost comprehensive dictionaries of English language on the market and extracted around eighteen,000 personality-describing words. From this list they reduced the amount of words to roughly four,500 temperament-describing adjectives that they thought of to explain noticeable and comparatively permanent personality traits.

Allport organized these traits into a hierarchy of 3 levels:

Cardinal traits dominate Associate in Nursingd form an individual's behavior, like Ebenezer Scrooge's greed or Mother Theresa's unselfishness. They stand at the highest of the hierarchy and ar jointly referred to as the individual's master management. they're thought of to be Associate in Nursing individual's ruling passions. Cardinal traits ar powerful, however few individuals have personalities dominated by one attribute. Instead, our personalities ar generally composed of multiple traits.

Central traits come back next within the hierarchy. These ar general characteristics found in variable degrees in all and sundry (such as loyalty, kindness, agreeableness, friendliness, sneakiness, wildness, or grouchiness). they're the essential building blocks that form most of our behavior.

Secondary traits exist at all-time low of the hierarchy and don't seem to be quite as obvious or consistent as central traits. {they ar|they're} plentiful however are solely gift below specific circumstances; they embody things like preferences and attitudes. These secondary traits justify why someone might sometimes exhibit behaviors that appear incongruent with their usual behaviors. as an example, a friendly person gets Associate in Nursinggry once individuals attempt to tickle him; another isn't an anxious person however continuously feels nervous speaking in public.

Allport hypothesized that internal Associate in Nursingd external forces influence an individual's behavior and temperament, and he stated these forces as genotypes and phenotypes. Genotypes ar internal forces that relate to however someone retains data and uses it to act with the globe. Phenotypes ar external forces that relate to the approach a personal accepts his or her surroundings and the way others influence his or her behavior.

Raymond Cattell (1905–1998)

In a trial to create Allport's list of four,500 traits additional manageable, Raymond Cattell took the list and removed all the synonyms, reducing the amount right down to 171. However, speech communication that a attribute is either gift or absent doesn't accurately replicate a person's individuation, as a result of (according to attribute theorists) all of our personalities are literally created from constant attributes; we have a tendency to take issue solely within the degree to that every trait is expressed.

Cattell believed it necessary to sample a large vary of variables to capture a full understanding of temperament. the primary kind of knowledge was life knowledge, that involves aggregation data from Associate in Nursing individual's natural existence behaviors. Experimental knowledge involves activity reactions to standardized experimental things, and form knowledge involves gathering responses supported thoughtfulness by a personal concerning his or her own behavior and feelings. exploitation this knowledge, Cattell performed correlational analysis to generated sixteen dimensions of human temperament traits: preoccupancy, warmth, apprehension, emotional stability, liveliness, openness to alter, disposition, privateness, intelligence , rule consciousness , tension, sensitivity, social boldness, independence, vigilance, and dominance.

Based on these sixteen factors, he developed a questionnaire referred to as the 16PF. rather than a attribute being gift or absent, every dimension is scored over a time, from high to low. as an example, your level heatth|of heat} describes however warm, caring, and nice to others you're. If you score low on this index, you tend to be additional distant and cold. A high score on this index signifies you're corroboratory and comforting. Despite reducing considerably on Allport's list of traits, Cattell's 16PF theory has still been criticized for being too broad.

Hans Eysenck (1916–1997)

Hans Eysenck was a temperament theorizer World Health Organization targeted on temperament—innate, genetically primarily based temperament variations. He believed temperament is essentially ruled by biology, and he viewed individuals as having 2 specific temperament dimensions: sociableness vs. introversion and psychological disorder vs. stability. once collaborating together with his married woman and fellow temperament theorizer Sybil H. J. Eysenck, he supplementary a 3rd dimension to the present model: psychoticism vs. socialization.

According to their theory, individuals high on the attribute of sociableness area unit sociable and outgoing and without delay connect with others, whereas individuals high on the attribute of introversion have the next have to be compelled to be alone, interact in solitary behaviors, and limit their interactions with others.

In the neuroticism/stability dimension, individuals high on psychological disorder tend to be associate degreexious; they have a tendency to possess an active sympathetic systema nervosum and even with low stress, their bodies and spirit tend to travel into a flight-or-fight reaction. In distinction, individuals high on stability tend to want additional stimulation to activate their flight-or-fight reaction and area unit so thought-about additional showing emotion stable.

Conclusion

The study of the theories of temperament is vital for college students because it prompts the requirement tounderstand why individuals behave as they are doing. Also, this space of study enlightens individuals on the requirement to be a lot of kind once judgement others supported however they behave since it's going to not be as a results of their own selection. The theories of privateity ar numerous relating to the character of personal behavior descriptions. additionally to the common theories, a reasonably uncommon conception, epigenetics is highlighted within the study of temperament theories. the range of personalities and therefore the relationships between the theories describing them points to the very fact that the human observation done by the theorists was correct to an oversized extent.

Personality is the collection of characteristic thoughts, feelings, and behaviors that make up a person. Human personality is a complex area of study. Not only is human nature complex, but also each individual has a unique combination of inherent abilities and preferences and learned responses. Beyond that, any researchers of personality also have certain personalities, which requires them to "bare their soul" in order to understand themselves and others.

CHAPTER FIFTEEN

Adjustment Concept Process Of Adjustment And Defence Mechanism

Introduction

In science, adjustment refers to the activity method by that humans and alternative animals accomplish a balance between their various needs or between their demands and therefore the difficulties in their circumstances. Once a necessity is felt, a series of changes begins and finishes with the satisfaction of that require. Hungry folks, as an example, ar compelled to hunt food by their state. They're acclimated to the current explicit demand after they eat as a result of the stimulating scenario that compelled them to action is reduced after they eat.

What is adjustment ?

The word "adjustment" comes from the word "adaptation" in biology. Biologists used the phrase "adaptation" to discuss with changes within the physical demands of the surroundings, whereas psychologists use the term "adjustment" to discuss with changes within the social or inter-personal relationships in society.

The individual's response to the stress and pressures of the social surroundings is noted as adjustment. The individual could also be needed to retort to associate external or internal demand.

Adjustment has been seen by psychologists from 2 perspectives: "adjustment as a goal" and "adjustment as a method."

Adjustment as achievement:

The term "adjustment as achievement" refers to a human ability to fulfil his job effectively in a very style of things. If we tend to contemplate adjustment to be a hit, we tend to should establish criteria to assess the standard of the adjustment. Psychologists have developed four criteria for judgment the adequacy of adjustment. the subsequent ar a number of them:

Physical well-being

Psychological ease

Efficiency within the work and

Acceptance in society

Adjustment as a process:

The phrase "adjustment as a process" emphasises the method by that an individual adjusts to his or her surroundings. It's essential, significantly from the attitude of academics. The degree to that students change is primarily determined by their interactions with the surroundings during which they live. They're perpetually trying to adapt to that. Jean Piaget checked out the adaptive method from a spread of views.

Assimilation and accommodation ar terms utilized by Jean Piaget to explain the method of adjusting oneself or one's surroundings.

Assimilator could be a one who retains his or her principles and standards of conduct no matter massive changes within the social atmosphere.

The term "accommodator" refers to somebody WHO adapts their concepts to the dynamic ideals of society by taking their standards from their social setting.

In order to with success integrate into society, an individual should use each devices, specifically assimilation and accommodation.

Characteristics of a well-adjusted person:

Some noticeable activity patterns ought to be gift in a very healthy and well-balanced person. These patterns of behaviour should be according to a human social expectations. the subsequent ar some samples of these patterns:

Imaginative maturity

Emotional equilibrium

Others ar treated with heat and thought.

Free from the strain of everyday occurrences

Making selections on your own

Elements in adjustment:

There ar many key factors for meeting the wants that ar needed for a human healthy adjustment. the subsequent ar the details:

Satisfaction of necessities

There is no impediment to meeting desires.

Strong motivations for meeting demands

Possibility of an appropriate geographical surroundings to satisfy desires

Mechanisms of adjustment

Individuals use 'adjustment mechanisms' to regulate to their surroundings, solve difficulties, and touch upon the anxiety-inducing and conflicting processes of life. Any habitual strategy of overcoming blockages, accomplishing goals, satisfying reasons, easing frustration, and associated conserving physiological condition will be classified as an adjustment mechanism. Every person depends on his or her own mechanisms to stay the balance of his or her adjustment at intervals and toward society under control.

Defense mechanism

Any of a group of mental processes that allows the mind to succeed in compromise solutions to disputes that it's unable to resolve, in keeping with psychotherapy theory. The compromise is sometimes unconscious, and it entails concealment internal urges or sensations that threaten to undermine shallowness or cause anxiety from oneself. the thought is predicated on the psychotherapy theory that there square measure opposing forces within the mind that fight one different. Sigmund Freud coined the term in his study "The Neuro-Psychoses of Defense" (1894).

The following square measure a number of the main defence mechanisms delineated by psychoanalysts:

1. Repression is that the method of golf stroke associate degree unwelcome plan, affect, or need into the unconscious space of the mind so as to get rid of it from consciousness. A instance of hysterical cognitive state, within which the victim performs or witnesses a terrible act and later on entirely forgets concerning it and therefore the circumstances encompassing it, is associate degree example.

2. Reaction creation is that the acutely aware concentration on associate degree opposing thought, mood, or need to a feared unconscious impulse. as an example, a mother World Health Organization bears associate degree unwanted child might react to her guilt for not needing the kid by changing into protective and solicitous so as to steer each the kid and herself that she could be a smart mother.

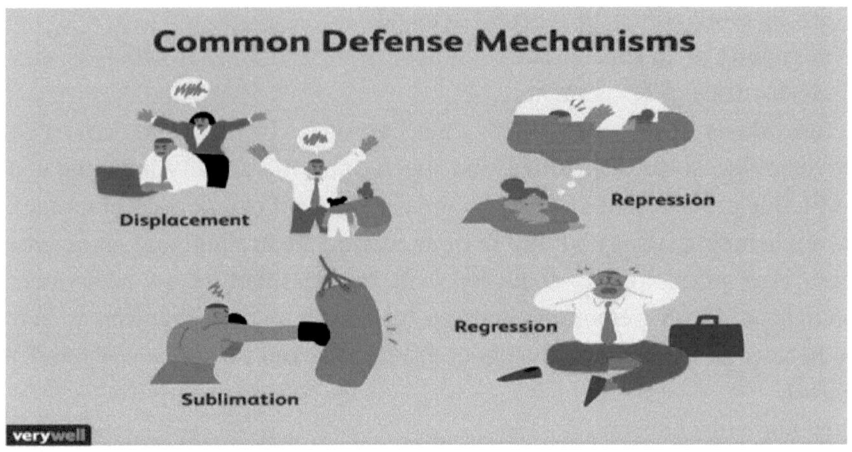

Source: very well

3. Projection could be a protecting mechanism within which unsought sentiments square measure projected onto another person, wherever they're perceived as a danger from the surface world. once a private is intimidated by his own furious feelings, he accuses another of harbouring hostile concepts, that could be a common sort of projection.

4. Regression could be a comeback to earlier stages of development and abandoned forms of pleasure that square measure related to them, triggered by dangers or conflicts that arise at one in all the later stages.

After her first dispute with her husband, a young wife can retire to the safety of her parents' house.

5. Sublimation is the redirection of instinctive desires, usually sexual ones, into non-instinctual channels. According to psychoanalytic thought, the energy spent on sexual desires can be diverted to more socially acceptable and even productive pursuits, such as artistic or scientific endeavours.

6. Denial is the deliberate reluctance to acknowledge the existence of uncomfortable realities. An individual can avoid intolerable ideas, feelings, or experiences by suppressing hidden feelings of homosexuality or animosity, or mental problems in one's child.

The deployment of a defence mechanism is a normal element of personality function, according to psychoanalysts, and is not an indication of psychiatric disease in and of itself. Excessive or strict employment of these defences, on the other hand, can be a symptom of a variety of psychological illnesses.

CONCLUSION

For one thing, adjustment is a goal, and for another, it is a process. The first highlights the effectiveness or quality of adjustment, while the second emphasises the process by which an individual adjusts to his external environment. Thus, healthy adjustment is a process in which an individual successfully achieves his biological, psychological, and social requirements while also establishing a balance between his inner wants and society's outward demands through appropriate behavioural reactions.

REFERENCES

https://www.britannica.com/science/photoperiodism

http://www.edugyan.in/2017/03/adjustment-maladjustment.html

https://www.britannica.com/topic/defense-mechanism

esearchgate.net/publication/
314087231_ADJUSTMENT_PROCESS_ACHEIVEMENT_
CHARACTERISTICS_MEASUREMENT_AND_DIMENSIONS

http://egyankosh.ac.in/bitstream/123456789/8519/1/Unit-16.pdf

https://www.indiastudychannel.com/resources/131499-Types-of-adjustment-in-Psychology.aspx

https://dictionary.apa.org/adjustment

https://en.wikipedia.org/wiki/Adjustment_(psychology)

https://www.simplypsychology.org/defense-mechanisms.html

https://nptel.ac.in/content/storage2/courses/109104070/Module-1.pdf

Printed by Libri Plureos GmbH in Hamburg,
Germany